NOTABLE AMERICAN UNITARIANS
1740-1900

by HERBERT F. VETTER

*Harvard Square Library book designed
by Andrew Drane and Lori Sellstrom*

Notable American Unitarians 1740-1900

This book is not copyrighted and is placed in the public domain by Harvard Square Library 2005, Cambridge, Massachusetts.

Published by Fenestra Books™
610 East Delano Street, Suite 104, Tucson, Arizona 85705 U.S.A.
www.fenestrabooks.com

International Standard Book Number: 1-58736-468-9
Library of Congress Control Number: 2004116842

TABLE OF CONTENTS

INTRODUCTION 9

1. SOURCES OF THE LIBERAL FAITH 11

The Pilgrims 11
Pastor John Robinson 12
John Winthrop 13
Sir Henry Vane 14
Sir Richard Saltonstall 15
Roger Williams 16
John Calvin 17
Jonathan Edwards 18
Charles Chauncy 19
Jonathan Mayhew 20
Ebenezer Gay 21
Samuel West (of New Bedford) 22
Jeremy Belknap 23
William Bentley 24
Ezra Ripley 25
James Freeman 26
Hosea Ballou 27
Noah Worcester 28
William Emerson 29
Joseph Stevens Buckminster 30
Jacobus (James) Arminius 31

2. GOVERNMENT 33

John Adams 33
Abigail Adams 34
John Quincy Adams 37
Charles Francis Adams 39
Thomas Jefferson 40
Millard Fillmore 41

Theophilus Parsons 43
Timothy Pickering 44
Joseph Story 46
Joseph Hodges Choate 47
Oliver Wendell Holmes, Jr. 48
Edward Everett 49
Charles Sumner 51
Daniel Webster 52
John C. Calhoun 53
Robert Gould Shaw 55
Josiah Quincy 56
George F. Hoar 57
Justin S. Morrill 58
George Bancroft 60

3. LITERATURE 63

Ralph Waldo Emerson 63
Henry Wadsworth Longfellow 65
Oliver Wendell Holmes 67
Louisa May Alcott 68
Nathaniel Hawthorne 70
James T. Fields 72
Herman Melville 73
George W. Curtis 75
Bret Harte 76
Margaret Fuller 77
William Ware 79
Richard Hildreth 80
Lydia Maria Francis Child 81
John Fiske 82
Francis Parkman 83
William Hickling Prescott 84

4. RELIGION 85

William Ellery Channing 85

Jared Sparks 87
Theodore Parker 88
Henry Ware, Sr. 89
Henry Ware, Jr. 90
Aaron Bancroft 92
Mary Safford 93
Thomas Starr King 96
Edward Everett Hale 97
John Pierpont 99
James Freeman Clarke 100
Charles Follen 102
Frederic Henry Hedge 104
Andrew Preston Peabody 105
Henry Whitney Bellows 107
Robert Collyer 108
Jenkin Lloyd Jones 110
Samuel McChord Crothers 112
Ezra Stiles Gannett 113
Antoinette Brown Blackwell 115
Octavius Brooks Frothingham .116
Francis Greenwood Peabody 117
Charles Carroll Everett 119
William Channing Gannett 120
Thomas Lamb Eliot 121
Samuel Atkins Eliot 124

5. SOCIAL CHANGE 125

Elizabeth Cady Stanton 125
Susan B. Anthony 127
Julia Ward Howe 128
Lucy Stone 130
Joseph Tuckerman 132
Josephine Shaw Lowell 134
Edwin D. Mead 136
Samuel Gridley Howe 137
Henry Bergh 138

Dorothea Dix 139
Samuel J. May 141
Charles Henry Appleton Dall 142
Jabez T. Sunderland 143

6. EDUCATION 145

Nine Unitarian Presidents of Harvard 145
Horace Mann 146
Mary Tyler Peabody Mann 148
Elizabeth Palmer Peabody 149
Booker T. Washington 151
Amory Dwight Mayo 152
Charles William Eliot 153
William Greenleaf Eliot 155
George Ticknor 157
John Lowell, Jr. 158

7. ARTS 161

Daniel Chester French 161
Charles Bulfinch: Architect of the Capitol 162
Fanny Kemble 164
Charlotte Cushman 166
Harriet Hosmer 167
Samuel Longfellow 168

8. SCIENCE 169

Maria Mitchell 169
Joseph Priestley 170
Louis Agassiz 172
Nathaniel Bowditch 173
Benjamin Athrop Gould 174
James Jackson, MD: Medical Science Pioneer 175
Jeffries Wyman: Naturalist 177
Asaph Hall: Discoverer of the Moons of Mars 178

Benjamin Peirce 179
Percival Lowell 180

9. BUSINESS 183

Abbott Lawrence 183
Amos Lawrence 184
Enoch Pratt 185
Jonas G. Clark 186
Harrison Gray Otis 187
Peter Cooper 188
John Murray Forbes: 190
Railroad Pioneer and Abolitionist
Thomas H. Perkins: 192
Merchant Prince of Boston
Ezra Cornell 193

ENDNOTE 195

Alphabetical Index of Names 196

INTRODUCTION

"American Unitarianism's great book" is the citation penned in 1923 to celebrate George Willis Cooke's *Unitarianism in America: Its Origin and Development*, published by the American Unitarian Association (AUA) in 1902.

A brief biography of the author—*George Willis Cooke*, by Charles A. Howe—is online in the *Dictionary of Unitarian Universalist Biography*.

This book necessarily has the limitations and prejudices of its period. It also expresses the personal style of the author in its inclusion of long lists of people he esteemed as important contributors to civilization. Nevertheless, Sydney Ahlstrom, the historian who documented Unitarianism in *An American Reformation*, concluded in 1985 that he had found Cooke's book the most adequate chronicle of events. Our presentation accepts the identification by the American Unitarian Association (AUA) and the author of people named as Unitarians, even though the listing may be imperfect now.

George Willis Cooke's celebration, at the beginning of the twentieth century, of the 75th anniversary of the American Unitarian Association—which was founded in 1825—was followed by several later publications. In 1925 the 100th anniversary of the AUA was observed with the publication by Beacon Press of *Our Unitarian Heritage* by Earl Morse Wilbur of the Starr King School for the Ministry in Berkeley, California. This book, which was prepared at the request of the AUA Department of Education for the use of young people, contained eighty pages in four chapters on "Unitarianism in America."

In 1952, volume two of *The History of Unitarianism*, Wilbur's *magnum opus,* was published by Harvard University. Though concentrated on Europe, it did include a section on America. However, Wilbur's story ends in 1900 and was not identified as celebrating the 125th anniversary of the American Unitarian Association.

The 150th anniversary of the AUA was celebrated in a well-illustrated book—*A Stream of Light: A Sesquicentennial History of American Unitarianism*—published by the Unitarian Universalist Association and edited by Conrad Wright, the historically unexcelled historian of Unitarianism in America. The Professor of American Church History at Harvard invited four other scholars to unite with him in telling the story: Charles Forman, Daniel Walker Howe, David B. Parke, and Carol R. Morris. This book is the most adequate and the most meticulously accurate tale of this liberal religious denomination.

Notable American Unitarians, begun online in 2000, is a celebration of Unitarianism by the First Parish in Cambridge, Massachusetts. Sustaining support has come from the Unitarian Universalist Funding Program of the Unitarian Universalist Association and from various cosponsors of the project. Cosponsors are: Unitarian Church of All Souls, New York, N.Y.; First Unitarian Society, Madison, WI; The First and Second Church of Boston; The First Parish in Cambridge; Unity Church - Unitarian in St. Paul, MN; The First Unitarian Universalist Church of Austin, TX; The Evangelical Missionary Society in Massachusetts, Weston; The Follen Church Society, Lexington, MA; The James Luther Adams Foundation; The Main Line Unitarian Church, Devon, PA; Freda Carnes, One Anonymous, Jan and Lowell Steinbrenner, and the A. Powell Davies Memorial Fund of All Souls Church, Washington, D.C.

Project advisors are Gloria Korsman, Andover-Harvard Theological Library; Conrad Edick Wright, Massachusetts Historical Society; and Conrad Wright, Harvard Divinity School. *Notable American Unitarians 1740-1800*

A color illustrated edition of this book is available on line at www.harvardsquarelibrary.org. *Likewise online is a full text of this abridged book, Notable American Unitarians 1936-1961.*

Herbert F. Vetter
Cambridge 2007

1. Sources of the Liberal Faith

THE PILGRIMS

The Mayflower and Plymouth Plantation
1620

The Mayflower at Sea
Courtesy of Pilgrim Hall Museum

The Mayflower carried 102 Pilgrims from England to Plymouth, Massachusetts, where they established New England's first permanent settlement in 1620.

Pastor John Robinson

1576(?)-1625

No actual portrait of Robinson exists; this is a substitute.

Pastor John Robinson's message to the Pilgrims departing from Amsterdam: "The Lord has more truth yet to break forth out of his holy word."

JOHN WINTHROP

1588-1649

Portrait in the Massachusetts State House

John Winthrop, who sailed on the Arbella in 1630, was governor of the Puritan colony of Massachusetts Bay until his death. He wrote *The History of New England* (two volumes), which he began on the Arbella.

SIR HENRY VANE

1589-1654

Elected governor of Massachusetts in 1636 Sir Henry Vane urged religious liberty and tolerance.

SIR RICHARD SALTONSTALL

1586-1658

A member of the Massachusetts Bay Company, Sir Richard Saltonstall sailed on the Arbella with John Winthrop to Salem in 1629. He continued his interest in the colony after returning to England in 1631.

ROGER WILLIAMS

1603-1683

Courtesy of the Library of Congress

The founder of Rhode Island was fiercely persecuted by William Laud, the Church of England's Archbishop of Canterbury. Williams and his wife sailed to Massachusetts Bay in 1631, and he became minister of the church in Salem. His persistent disagreements led the General Court to banish him from the colony. Williams escaped deportation by traveling during a blizzard to a place he named Providence, where a lively experiment in religious freedom led Rhode Islanders to establish what Williams considered appropriate relations between church and state.

JOHN CALVIN

1509-1564

Calvin was the French Protestant theologian who wrote the *Institutes of the Christian Religion* in 1536. When he moved to Geneva, he established a theocracy in which presbyters defined the faith and practice of the people.

Conrad Wright says that Calvin may properly be regarded as a figure in our family tree and important in shaping our history—by reaction. He set the questions to which our eighteenth-century ancestors gave non-Calvinist answers. The one who sets the frame of the debate is a dominating influence, so Calvin shaped our development.

JONATHAN EDWARDS

1703-1758

This unforgettable minister and philosophical theologian is best known for his single sermon describing God's wrath: "Sinners in the Hands of an Angry God." In this notable sermon, Edwards preached that the sinner was held tenuously over the abyss of hell like a spider on a web. Revulsion against his preaching and writing long promoted the advance of Unitarianism.

Jonathan Edwards was a pivotal American Calvinist who described and promoted religious revivals since he thought they might signal the coming of the millennium.

A whole library of volumes written by and about Edwards continue to be published anew. He was frequently afflicted with illnesses such as depression, likely allied with social rejection.

Charles Chauncy

1705-1787

Courtesy of the Unitarian Universalist Association

Charles Chauncy, the great-grandson of the minister who came to Plymouth in 1638, became the second president of Harvard College, and served the First Church in Boston for sixty years, effectively opposing Jonathan Edwards and the extravagant emotionalism of the Great Awakening. He was not only an advocate of the American Revolution, but also a public champion of the doctrines of universalism. Chauncy was a precursor of Unitarianism.

JONATHAN MAYHEW

1720-1766

Courtesy of Old West Church, Boston

Mayhew's father was a Congregational missionary to Indians, whereas Jonathan served for nineteen years as minister of the West Congregational Church of Boston, which the orthodox suspected of liberal tendencies. Their suspicion was confirmed when Dr. Gay of Hingham preached the ordination sermon.

A successor described Jonathan Mayhew as "the first preacher in Boston of an antitrinitarian God, the most clerical asserter in America of civil and religious affairs who broke down the partition wall between secular and religious affairs."

EBENEZER GAY

1696-1787

Courtesy of William Wiltshire, Richmond, Virginia

The pastor of Hingham's "Old Ship" church for sixty-nine years, Ebenezer Gay, actively opposed the Great Awakening revivalist, George Whitefield.

In directly attacking Calvinism, he positively affirmed human ability and freedom.

Samuel West (of New Bedford)

1730-1807

Mural in the Massachusetts State House

This influential minister was a member of the committee that framed the Constitution of Massachusetts, and in 1776 he preached before the Massachusetts Council and House of Representatives in Boston on "The Right to Rebel Against Governors."

JEREMY BELKNAP

1744-1798

Courtesy of the University of Virginia Library

Jeremy Belknap is known as the founder of the Massachusetts Historical Society, America's prototype for such organizations. He ministered in Dover, New Hampshire, and Boston, Massachusetts. In 1775 he was chaplain for American troops in Cambridge.

His writings include a *History of New Hampshire, 1784-92* and *A Discourse Intended to Commemorate the Discovery of America by Columbus*. Alexis de Tocqueville declared Belknap America's best native historian.

WILLIAM BENTLEY

1759-1819

Courtesy of the Pelletier Library, Allegheny College, Meadville, Pennsylvania

Bentley was the minister of the Second Church in Salem, Massachusetts, for thirty-six years. He was famous for his encyclopedic knowledge and was a Unitarian opponent of intolerant evangelical Calvinists. He never married. His unique library, one of the largest of his day, contained at least 4,000 volumes.

EZRA RIPLEY

1751-1841

Courtesy of the Unitarian Universalist Association

Ripley was the minister of the First Parish in Concord, Massachusetts; chief citizen of the town; step-grandfather of Ralph Waldo Emerson; and cofounder in Concord of America's first lyceum. Ordained a Trinitarian Calvinist, he became a Unitarian.

JAMES FREEMAN

1759-1835

Courtesy of the Unitarian Universalist Association

James Freeman was the minister of King's Chapel, Boston, the Anglican congregation that voted in 1785 to delete references to the Trinity in the Book of Common Prayer. King's Chapel was the first church to publicly adopt the Unitarian view.

HOSEA BALLOU

1771-1852

Courtesy of Tufts Magazine

Hosea Ballou's great-great-grandfather was a coproprietor with Roger Williams of Rhode Island in 1646. His mother died when he was twenty months old. His father was a frontier farmer who ministered without pay. There was no school in Richmond, New Hampshire, but Hosea educated himself. When he asked his Baptist father if an inanimate substance were made animate would it suffer everlasting misery, his father told Hosea that he would have to answer his own question.

The family migrated to Massachusetts, and Hosea studied the Bible and chose to become a minister preaching the gospel of universal salvation for all as a circuit rider. He became the pastor of the Second Universalist Church in Boston from 1817 until his death in 1852, and he was also founder and editor of *The Universalist Magazine*. His primary book, *A Treatise on the Atonement* (1805), proclaimed that a God of love would not condemn us to eternal punishment.

NOAH WORCESTER

1758-1837

Courtesy of the Unitarian Universalist Association

Born in Hollis, New Hampshire, Worcester was at sixteen a fifer with the American revolutionary forces at Bunker Hill. By the age of twenty he was writing intently in response to theological questions while working as a shoemaker. When he was given a license to preach as a Congregational minister, he served at a Thornton, New Hampshire church to support his large family. His salary of $200 a year (if paid) was supplemented by farming and making shoes.

When condemned for his Unitarian views, he was invited by William Ellery Channing to become editor of the *Christian Disciple*. For five years this was his pivotal Unitarian ministry. He was also the founder of the Massachusetts Peace Society, which opposed war and spawned the American Peace Society. Harvard College awarded him an honorary doctorate.

WILLIAM EMERSON

1768-1811

Courtesy of the Concord Free Library

The father of Ralph Waldo Emerson, William Emerson was the minister of the First Church in Boston. He was a founder of the Anthology Club, a Boston literary society that included George Ticknor and Daniel Webster, and he wrote articles for the club's *The Monthly Anthology*. Their publication was the forerunner of *The North American Review*, America's leading literary journal. The Anthology Club's reading room led to the founding in 1807 of the Boston Athenaeum.

Joseph Stevens Buckminster

1784-1812

Courtesy of the Unitarian Universalist Association

Buckminster was an early leader in bringing the German higher criticism of the Bible to America. He was also the most eloquent of the early liberal preachers in Boston. After graduating from Harvard in 1800, he was called to the Brattle Street Church in Boston and launched an almost legendary career of eloquent preaching, biblical scholarship, and literary production. He, in many ways, set the tone for the pattern of the minister as a man of letters, a pattern which prevailed in nineteenth-century Boston Unitarianism. Buckminster preached a distinctly liberal message of rational religion and character development, themes that his contemporary, William Ellery Channing, would later develop. He also influenced the denomination heavily in his adoption of the attitude of rational investigation of the Bible, subjecting it to the same scrupulous scholarly investigation given other texts from antiquity. Buckminster suffered an early death from epilepsy when his powers were only reaching their height.

JACOBUS (JAMES) ARMINIUS

1560-1609

Arminius, a Dutch teacher at the University of Leiden, repudiated the Calvinistic dogma of God's predestination of each individual to either endless bliss in heaven or eternal suffering in hell. Arminius said there is no freedom where there is no power to choose. Such a God would be evil—an absolute tyrant, the opposite of love.

Historian Conrad Wright notes, however, that "his influence on the eighteenth century was remote," and they did not get their rejection of Calvinism from reading him.

2. Government

JOHN ADAMS

1735-1826

Portrait in the Smithsonian's National Portrait Gallery

The second president of the United States, Adams was a lawyer who fostered the American Revolution and served in both the First Continental Congress in 1774 and the Second Continental Congress in 1775. At the Second Continental Congress, John Adams seconded the nomination of George Washington as commander-in-chief of the Continental Army. In another bold, historically defining recommendation, he supported Thomas Jefferson's selection as author of the Declaration of Independence in 1776.

John Adams wrote the Constitution of the Commonwealth of Massachusetts, which became the model for the Constitution of the United States.

John Adams and Thomas Jefferson both died on the same day: July 4, 1826. Adams's final resting place is in the crypt of the United First Parish Church (Unitarian), Quincy, Massachusetts.

ABIGAIL ADAMS

1744-1818

Courtesy of the White House Historical Association

Inheriting New England's strongest traditions, Abigail Smith was born in 1744 in Weymouth, Massachusetts. On her mother's side she was descended from the Quincys, a family of great prestige in the colony; her father and other forebears were Congregational ministers, leaders in a society that held its clergy in high esteem.

Like other women of the time, Abigail lacked formal education; but her curiosity spurred her keen intelligence, and she read avidly the books at hand. Reading created a bond between her and John Adams—a young Harvard graduate launching a career in law—and they were married in 1764. It was a marriage of the mind and of the heart, and it endured for more than half a century, enriched by time. The young couple lived on John's small farm at Braintree or in Boston as his practice expanded. In ten years she bore three sons and two daughters; she looked after family and home when he went traveling as circuit judge. "Alas!" she wrote in December 1773, "How many snow banks divide thee and me…"

Long separations kept Abigail from her husband while he served the country they loved as delegate to the Continental

Congress, envoy abroad, and elected officer under the Constitution. Her letters—pungent, witty, and vivid, spelled just as she spoke—detail her life in times of revolution. They tell the story of the woman who stayed at home to struggle with wartime shortages and inflation, who ran the farm with a minimum of help, and who taught her four children when their formal education was interrupted. Most of all, they tell of her loneliness without her "dearest Friend." The "one single expression," she said, "dwelt upon my mind and played about my Heart ..."

In 1784, she joined John at his diplomatic post in Paris, where she observed with interest the manners of the French. After 1785, she filled the difficult role of wife of the first United States Minister to Great Britain, and did so with dignity and tact. They returned happily in 1788 to Massachusetts and the handsome house they had just acquired in Braintree, later called Quincy, their home for the rest of their lives.

As wife of the first vice president, Abigail became a good friend to Mrs. Washington and a valued help in official entertaining, drawing on her experience of courts and society abroad. After 1791, poor health forced her to spend as much time as possible in Quincy. Illness or trouble found her resolute; as she once declared, she would "not forget the blessings which sweeten life."

When John Adams was elected president, she continued a formal pattern of entertaining—even in the primitive conditions she found at the new capital in November 1800. The city was a wilderness, the President's House far from completion. Her private complaints to her family provide blunt accounts of both, but for her three months in Washington she duly held her dinners and receptions.

The Adamses retired to Quincy in 1801, and for seventeen years enjoyed the companionship that public life had long denied them. Abigail died in 1818, and she is buried beside her husband in United First Parish Church. She leaves her country a most remarkable record as patriot and First Lady, wife of one President and mother of another. To the latter, John Quincy Adams, she wrote in a letter dated May 5, 1816: "There is not any reasoning which can convince me, contrary to my senses, that three is one and one three. I acknowledge myself a Unitarian …"

John Quincy Adams

1767-1848

Courtesy of the Library of Congress

The first president who was the son of a president, John Quincy Adams in many respects paralleled the career, as well as the temperament and viewpoints, of his illustrious father. Born in Braintree, Massachusetts, in 1767, Adams watched the Battle of Bunker Hill as a young boy from the top of Penn's Hill above the family farm. As secretary to his father in Europe, he became an accomplished linguist and assiduous diarist.

After graduating from Harvard College, he became a lawyer. At age twenty-six he was appointed minister to the Netherlands, and he was later part of the Berlin Legation. He was elected to the United States Senate in 1802. Six years later, President Madison appointed him minister to Russia.

Serving under President Monroe, Adams was one of America's great secretaries of state, arranging with England for the joint occupation of the Oregon country, obtaining from Spain the cession of the Floridas, and formulating with the president the Monroe Doctrine.

Upon becoming president, Adams appointed Henry Clay secretary of state. Andrew Jackson and his angry followers charged that a "corrupt bargain" had taken place and immediately began their campaign to wrest the presidency from Adams in 1828.

Well aware that he would face hostility in Congress, Adams nevertheless proclaimed in his first annual message a spectacular national program. He proposed that the federal government bring the nation together with a network of highways and canals, and that it develop and conserve the public domain, using funds from the sale of public lands.

The campaign of 1828, in which his Jacksonian opponents charged him with corruption and public plunder, was an ordeal Adams did not endure easily. After his defeat, he returned to Massachusetts, expecting to spend the remainder of his life enjoying his farm and his books.

Unexpectedly, in 1830, the Plymouth district elected him to the House of Representatives, and there for the remainder of his life he served as a powerful leader. Above all, he fought against circumscription of civil liberties. He fought against the gag rule that had been adopted by the House of Representatives to stop the flood of antislavery petitions being introduced by him.

In 1848, he collapsed on the floor of the House from a stroke and was carried to the Speaker's Room, where two days later he died. He was buried—as were his father, mother, and wife—at First Parish Church in Quincy. To the end, "Old Man Eloquent" had fought for what he considered right.

Adapted from the whitehouse.gov biography. Both John Quincy Adams and John C. Calhoun were founders of All Souls Unitarian Church in Washington, D.C.

CHARLES FRANCIS ADAMS

1807-1886

From The Boston Athenaeum Centenary, The Boston Athenaeum, *1908*

An American diplomat—and the son of President John Quincy Adams—Charles Francis Adams traveled in his youth with his parents to St. Petersburg when his father was the United States minister to Russia. After reading law in the office of Daniel Webster, he won office in the Massachusetts General Court, the U.S. House of Representatives, and the Senate. When appointed by Abraham Lincoln as minister to Great Britain during the Civil War, he helped to end the British building of commerce raiders destined to provide arms for the Confederate Navy.

Adams wrote a two-volume biography of his grandfather, John Adams, as well as the *Memoirs of John Quincy Adams*. His own biography, as part of the "American Statesmen Series," was written by his son, Charles Francis Adams, Jr.

THOMAS JEFFERSON

1743-1826

Courtesy of the National Portrait Gallery, Smithsonian Institution

The author of the Declaration of Independence was President Washington's secretary of state before he himself became a vice president—and ultimately president of the newly formed United States.

In 1803, Jefferson's purchase of Louisiana doubled the size of the Union and enabled the American expansion that characterized much of the nineteenth century.

Jefferson cherished his role as the author of the Virginia Statute for Religious Freedom, as well as his role as the founder of the University of Virginia.

An architect by training, who designed his own home, he retired as the "Sage of Monticello."

For eighteen years he was the president of the American Philosophical Society.

One expression of his Unitarian faith was his compilation of *The Life and Morals of Jesus of Nazareth*, sometimes called *The Jefferson Bible*. He is also remembered for saying, "I trust there is not a young man now living who will not die a Unitarian."

MILLARD FILLMORE

1800-1874

Courtesy of the White House

Born in the Finger Lakes country of New York in 1800, Fillmore as a youth endured the privations of frontier life. He worked on his father's farm and at fifteen was apprenticed to a cloth dresser. He attended one-room schools and fell in love with a redheaded teacher, Abigail Powers, who later became his wife.

In 1823, he was admitted to the bar; seven years later he moved his law practice to Buffalo. As an associate of the Whig politician Thurlow Weed, Fillmore held state office and for eight years was a member of the House of Representatives. In 1848, while comptroller of New York, he was elected vice president.

Fillmore presided over the Senate during the months of nerve-wracking debates over the Compromise of 1850. He made no public comment on the merits of the compromise proposals, but a few days before President Zachary Taylor's death, he intimated to him that if there should be a tie vote on Henry Clay's bill, he would vote in favor of it.

Thus the sudden accession of Fillmore to the presidency in July 1850 brought an abrupt political shift in the administration. Taylor's Cabinet resigned, and President Fillmore at once appointed Daniel Webster to be secretary of state, thus proclaiming his alliance with the moderate Whigs who favored the Compromise.

THEOPHILUS PARSONS

1750-1813

Courtesy of the Social Law Library, Boston

President John Quincy Adams prepared for legal practice in the office of Theophilus Parsons. Known for his patriotism, Parsons advocated the adoption of the Massachusetts State Constitution and supported the ratification of the federal Constitution. Parsons and John Hancock secured three amendments to the Constitution, thereby adding them to the Bill of Rights.

When he moved to Boston in 1800, Parsons became chief justice of the Supreme Judicial Court of Massachusetts, establishing a tradition of excellence. The court developed corporate law practices that have been cited as the legal foundation of American capitalist enterprise.

TIMOTHY PICKERING

1745-1829

Courtesy of the U.S. Army Center of Military History

George Washington appointed Pickering adjutant general, and then as quartermaster of the army. He was a representative in the Pennsylvania delegation that ratified the Constitution of the United States.

Here is a U.S. State Department profile:

Born: July 17, 1745
Died: January 29, 1829
Married: Rebecca White
Education: Harvard College
Occupation: Lawyer

Government Positions:

- Entered Revolutionary Army as colonel in 1775
- Elected to state legislature in 1776
- Appointed Adjutant General, 1777
- Elected member of the Board of War, 1777
- Quartermaster General of the Army, 1780-1785

- Organized Luzerne County, Pennsylvania, and represented it in the convention of 1787 that ratified the Federal Constitution and in the state constitutional convention of 1789-1790
- Postmaster General, 1791-1795
- Secretary of War in President Washington's Cabinet in 1795
- Secretary of State ad interim, August 20-December 9, 1795
- Chief Justice of the Massachusetts Court of Common Pleas in 1802
- Senator for Massachusetts, 1803-1800
- Member of State Executive Council, 1812-1813
- Representative from Massachusetts, 1813-1817

JOSEPH STORY

1779-1845

From Louis D. Brandeis, The Harvard Law School (1889)

President Madison appointed Story—at the age of thirty-two—to the U.S. Supreme Court in 1811. In 1829, Story became the first Dane Professor of Law at Harvard Law School, and he continued to hold both positions throughout the remainder of his life. An ally of Chief Justice John Marshall in advocacy of strong federal law, he not only brought Harvard Law School to national primacy but also wrote many volumes shaping the development of American law, including his *Commentaries on the Constitution.*

JOSEPH HODGES CHOATE

1832-1917

Courtesy of the Collections of the New York Genealogical and Biographical Society

This lawyer, who grew up in Salem, Massachusetts, battled the political Tammany Society in New York before he became U.S. ambassador to Great Britain. He settled the Alaska-Canada dispute and negotiated the Open Door Policy in China.

In addition to his service as founder of the American Museum of Natural History, Choate strengthened New York's Metropolitan Museum of Art, New York Hospital, and the Carnegie Endowment for International Peace.

He was an advocate of laissez-faire economic policy. Some people did not forget that, even during a great U.S. depression, Choate vigorously attacked the income tax as a form of class warfare.

OLIVER WENDELL HOLMES, JR.

1841-1935

Courtesy of the Library of Congress

The grandson of the Reverend Abiel Holmes and son of the famous poet, Holmes responded to the call of President Lincoln for 75,000 volunteers during the Civil War. Captain Holmes was wounded three times, twice almost fatally. Upon recovering, he and William James spent long nights discussing their "dilapidated old friend the Kosmos."

After studying and practicing law, he published his Lowell Lectures as *The Common Law*, long cited as the greatest work of American legal scholarship. His first sentence is, "The life of the Law has been not logic but experience."

Following his twenty years' service as a member of the Supreme Judicial Court of Massachusetts, President Theodore Roosevelt appointed him to the U. S. Supreme Court, a post he held for thirty years before retirement at the age of ninety-one.

"The Great Dissenter" was buried with his wife, Fanny Bowditch Dixwell, at the Arlington National Cemetery.

EDWARD EVERETT

1794-1865

Edward Everett, after a painting by Alonzo Chappel, courtesy of the Library of Congress

After receiving Harvard degrees, Edward Everett became, in 1814, the minister of Boston's distinguished Brattle Street Church. In 1815, however, he accepted Harvard's offer to become the Eliot Professor of Greek Literature. Harvard provided funds for him to study at Göttingen University where, in 1817, he was the first American to receive a Ph.D.

In addition to teaching, he edited *The North American Review* of literature. Everett was Ralph Waldo Emerson's teacher and a model of eloquence.

He was elected to the U.S. House of Representatives, and went on to terms as governor of Massachusetts and U.S. secretary of state before becoming the president of Harvard for three years. After serving in the U.S. Senate, he toured the land as a famous orator celebrating America, especially George Washington.

After delivering an address at the dedication of the cemetery at Gettysburg before Abraham Lincoln spoke, Dr. Everett wrote to the president, "I should be glad if I could flatter myself that I came as near to the central idea of the occasion in two hours as you did in two minutes."

From the Executive Mansion came this reply: "Honorable Edward Everett. My dear Sir: I am pleased to know that, in your judgment, the little I did say was not entirely a failure. Of course, I knew Mr. Everett would not fail. Our sick boy, for whom you kindly inquire, we hope is past the worst. Your obedient Servant, A. Lincoln."

CHARLES SUMNER

1811-1874

Lithograph by Henry Schile, 1874, courtesy of the Library of Congress

A most prominent opponent of slavery, U.S. Senator Charles Sumner attacked slave power as an alliance between "the lords of the lash and the lords of the loom." A master orator without notes, he was likewise adept in facilitating the formation of the Republican Party in opposition to slavery.

His famous address on "The Crime of Slavery" released his rage against Senators Stephen Douglas of Illinois and Andrew Butler of South Carolina. Two days later, Congressman Preston Brooks of South Carolina attacked Sumner while he was seated at his desk, mercilessly beating him with his cane until he fell to the floor in bloody unconsciousness. The wounds were so severe it took three years of healing before Sumner returned to the Senate. His seat had been kept open by the grateful people of Massachusetts.

A confidante of President Lincoln, Sumner was influential in encouraging the Proclamation of Emancipation. He died when, against his doctor's advice, he went to the Senate on a day crucial for voting and suffered a terminal heart attack.

DANIEL WEBSTER

1782-1852

Courtesy of the National Portrait Gallery, Smithsonian Institution

John Lothrop Motley said, "Thinking of America without Webster seems like thinking of her without Niagara or the Mississippi."

Born in New Hampshire, Daniel Webster was a graduate of Dartmouth College, whose online exhibit describes the last days of this defender of the Constitution:

"Few have left such a lasting mark on all three branches of American government. Webster's cases before the Supreme Court are cited daily as the foundations of American contract and the supremacy of the Constitution over the states. The Webster-Ashburton Treaty and his work as secretary of state averted a third war with Great Britain, and ushered in a new era of peace. It remains a founding document in the law of nations. Webster's portrait appears no fewer than six times in the U.S. Capitol, a tribute to the man who three times averted civil war and epitomizes what is now called 'the Golden Age of Senate Oratory.' Lincoln later cited Webster's words as an important source of inspiration in guiding the nation through the Civil War. And if, as his critics contended, Webster sold his soul by compromising on slavery, he did so only to purchase a few more years of peace for a troubled nation and to preserve the Constitution and the Union he so dearly loved."

JOHN C. CALHOUN

1782-1850

Courtesy of the National Portrait Gallery, Smithsonian Institution

John C. Calhoun is remembered both as an American statesman and political philosopher. From 1811 until his death, Calhoun served in the federal government—as congressman, secretary of war, vice president, senator, secretary of state, and again as senator.

Born on March 18, 1782, in South Carolina, Calhoun was largely self-educated before entering Yale as a junior in 1801. After graduating with honors in 1804, he attended law school in Litchfield, Connecticut, and was admitted to the South Carolina bar in 1807.

Calhoun entered the U.S. Congress in 1811, and was among those young nationalists known as the War Hawks urging war with Great Britain. His proposals for strengthening the armed forces and financing the war led to Calhoun's appointment as secretary of war in James Monroe's cabinet.

In 1824, Calhoun was elected vice president under John Quincy Adams. By 1828 he had aligned himself with Andrew Jackson and was again elected to the vice presidency when Jackson won the presidency. Unfortunately, Jackson and

Calhoun had become bitter enemies by 1832, and Calhoun resigned as vice president to reenter the Senate.

During his terms as vice president, Calhoun turned away from nationalism to become a strong champion of states' rights. As the antislavery campaign grew in the North, Calhoun, who had merely tolerated slavery, became its strongest defender. In 1844, as secretary of state in John Tyler's administration, he negotiated a treaty for the annexation of Texas. This effectively preserved sectional balance in the Union by enlarging the area open to slavery.

Calhoun's last appearance in Congress was on March 7, 1850, as he heard and approved Daniel Webster's appeal for sectional peace. Three days earlier, too ill to speak, Calhoun sat in the Senate as his speech was read for him. He died in Washington on March 31, 1850.

Both John Quincy Adams and John C. Calhoun were founders of All Souls Unitarian Church in Washington, DC.

ROBERT GOULD SHAW

1837-1863

Courtesy of the Massachusetts State House

The bronze statue, *Colonel Robert Gould Shaw and the 54th Regiment Memorial*, designed by Augustus St. Gaudens, stands on the Boston Common, across the street from the Massachusetts State House and the Unitarian Universalist Association. It celebrates the first black regiment recruited in the North to fight in the Civil War.

A member of a prominent Unitarian Family, Shaw worked for two years at his uncle's mercantile firm in Manhattan but felt enslaved by the job. "I don't want to be a merchant or a doctor or a minister."

The young man considered his life a failure until, at the outbreak of the Civil War, he distinguished himself as a soldier. Though wounded twice, he loved the military and was assigned to raise and command the first regiment of black troops organized in a Northern state. When the troops were trained, he volunteered to lead an assault on Fort Wagner, a Confederate stronghold in Charleston, South Carolina. Shaw was one of the 272 who were killed, wounded, or captured. His body was stripped of its uniform, and he was placed on display in the fort before being thrown in the bottom of a large pit, with the bodies of his comrades thrown on top of the martyr.

JOSIAH QUINCY

1772-1864

From The Memorial History of Boston, 1630-1880, *Vol.3*

Josiah Quincy graduated from Harvard in 1790, studied law, and was admitted to the bar in 1793. He served in the Massachusetts Senate in 1805, and from 1805 to 1813 was a member of the national House of Representatives. After leaving Congress, he held various political offices until he became mayor of Boston in 1823. As mayor, he brought about municipal reform, and in 1829 he resigned to become president of Harvard College. He remained president until 1845, during which time he made many reforms in grading and finances. His last years were spent on his farm in Quincy, where he died on July 1, 1864.

Edited by Justin Winsor, Boston, 1882.

George F. Hoar

1826-1904

Bust of Senator Hoar in the Massachusetts State House

Born in Concord, Massachusetts, Hoar practiced law in Worcester, Massachusetts, and served in the House of Representatives, where he actively advocated public education as a national agent of social transformation. After being elected to the U.S. Senate, he served for twenty years on the Senate Judiciary Committee and claimed authorship of the Sherman Antitrust Act of 1890.

An anti-imperialist, he was almost alone in seeking self-determination for both Filipinos and Puerto Ricans.

George Hoar twice declined a seat on the Supreme Court of the United States.

He died in Worcester, where he was a prominent Unitarian.

JUSTIN S. MORRILL

1810-1898

Portrait in the Senate Wing of the United States Capitol

Morrill was the driving force behind both the 1862 and 1890 U.S. Congress's creation of land grant universities in every state. While considered the greatest education legislation in U.S. history, passage of Morrill's College Land Bill was far from certain and deeply controversial. During congressional debates in 1859, James Mason of Virginia labeled the bill "one of the most extraordinary engines of mischief," a misuse of federal property, and "an unconstitutional robbing of the Treasury for the purpose of bribing the States." Ohio Congressman George Pugh said the bill involved "as atrocious a violation of the organic law as if it were the act of an armed usurper."

In hindsight, it's hard to believe that such a far-thinking, visionary, and beneficial legislative proposal could have engendered such bitter opposition. There was wide support among voters for the bill, but Southern states were vehemently opposed to Morrill's proposal. President Buchanan finally vetoed it at the urging of a group of Democratic senators led by John Slidell of Louisiana. With this veto, the bill was effectively dead until after the 1860 election.

With the election of Lincoln, prospects for passage improved, although pressing Civil War matters took precedence. Morrill introduced the bill in December 1860, but opposition in the House, this time from Western states, delayed consideration for six months. Meanwhile, friends in the Senate moved a version of the bill and won approval, even though Kansas and Minnesota opposed the "college land bill" as a dangerous giveaway to land speculators. After several attempts to delay and amend the bill in the House, it finally passed, and President Lincoln signed it into law on July 2, 1862.

Morrill was a staunch Republican. A fiscal conservative, he opposed large government surpluses and overtaxation; opposed Congressional pay raises, actually giving back his raise to the Vermont treasury; voted for a guilty verdict at the impeachment trial of a president; and championed the needs of his rural constituency.

But in other ways, Morrill was clearly a man of his own times. He opposed women's suffrage, opposed the eight-hour workday, and supported a movement to incorporate Canada into the United States.

Morrill, however, is best remembered for his efforts to provide federally supported education to the common people and to ensure that emancipated slaves would have access to the same educational opportunities as others.

By Kirk A. Astroth, Montana State University

GEORGE BANCROFT

1800-1891

Courtesy of the National Portrait Gallery, Smithsonian Institution

Bancroft's father, a minister in Worcester, Massachusetts, served as president of the American Unitarian Association.

George was a student in Göttingen, Germany, where he earned a doctorate in 1820. While in Europe, his exposure to current thinkers was rich. He heard Hegel and Schleiermacher speak in Berlin and personally met Goethe and Lafayette.

After trying a ministerial career, which he concluded would lead him nowhere, he briefly taught Greek at Harvard before initiating a path-breaking progressive education at Round Hill School in Northhampton, Massachusetts. Bancroft was dissatisfied with this achievement, and he soon moved on.

After marrying Sarah Dwight in 1827, he began writing his multi-volume *History of the United States*, a text that continued to sell well as the number of volumes grew.

He decided to enter politics. Although sustaining losses in local elections, he was propelled into national politics as secretary of the Navy. Bancroft established the Naval Academy in Annapolis, gave the orders that led to the occupation of California, and pleaded for the annexation of Texas.

His career as an American diplomat involved his being ambassador to Great Britain and serving as the U.S. minister to Prussia. He served in Berlin for seven years before he died in 1891.

3. Literature

RALPH WALDO EMERSON

1803-1882

Courtesy of the Library of Congress

Born in Boston, Waldo was one of the eight children of William Emerson, the eminent minister of the First Church in Boston. Upon the death of his father when Waldo was eight, his mother fought against poverty by taking in borders.

After attending Harvard College and Harvard Divinity School, Emerson became the minister of the Second Church in Boston (Unitarian). When he could not in good conscience conduct the Lord's Supper, he resigned in 1832 and moved to Concord to write.

In 1836, his first book, *Nature*, initiated a new movement, Transcendentalism, which fostered a renaissance of American literature and life, rooted in the affirmation: "The currents of the Universal Being circulate through me; I am part or parcel of God."

Emerson's 1837 Harvard Phi Beta Kappa address on "The American Scholar" Oliver Wendell Holmes proclaimed as

America's Declaration of Intellectual Independence. "We have listened too long to the courtly muses of Europe," Emerson said and predicted that America would become the pole star for a thousand years. "A nation of men will for the first time exist because each believes himself inspired by the Divine Soul."

At his Divinity School Address, delivered in 1838, hearers were urged to acquaint themselves firsthand with deity. This radical Christian critic of "corpse cold Unitarianism" also declared that "miracle is monster." Andrews Norton, Professor of Biblical Literature, branded Emerson's work "the latest form of infidelity." Ralph Waldo Emerson was not invited back to Harvard for thirty years.

The speaker was not exempt from tragedy. Loss of his first wife, aged nineteen, was followed by a son's death after Emerson remarried. Rheumatism and poor eyesight plagued him, but he persisted in delivering lectures near and far, as well as writing poems, essays, letters, and his diary, all grandly celebrated in 2003, the bicentennial of his birth. "The Sage of Concord" has been recognized as the most important figure in America's cultural renaissance of the nineteenth century.

HENRY WADSWORTH LONGFELLOW

1807-1882

Courtesy of the Library of Congress

This long-beloved poet, whose first American ancestor arrived from England in 1676, taught modern European languages at Bowdoin College and then at Harvard. While he and his young wife were visiting Europe, she died in Rotterdam. After he returned to Cambridge, he rented lodging at Craigie House, which had been General George Washington's headquarters during the Revolutionary War. Later, Henry married Fanny Appleton. Six children were born to them in Craigie House, which had been given to them by Fanny's father, a wealthy Bostonian. Fanny died a tragic death when she burned to death after hot sealing wax ignited her dress.

Resigning his Harvard chair in 1854, Longfellow devoted his life to writing. His literary legacy includes *The Song of Hiawatha, The Courtship of Miles Standish, Tales of a Wayside Inn,* and *Evangeline.* He also translated Dante's *Divine Comedy* into English.

This American Unitarian poet was honored by Queen Victoria, Oxford University, Cambridge University, the Russian Academy of Sciences, and the Spanish Academy. His brother Samuel, a Unitarian minister, wrote the authorized biography of Henry Wadsworth Longfellow in two volumes.

OLIVER WENDELL HOLMES

1809-1894

Courtesy of the National Library of Medicine

The Autocrat of the Breakfast Table named the *Atlantic Monthly* magazine, to which he regularly contributed articles of light humor. His first published poem, "Old Ironsides," successfully protested the proposed scrapping of the warship *Constitution*. His poem "The Deacon's Masterpiece" is a rollicking Unitarian critique of Calvinistic religion.

Dr. Holmes was a dominant member of the Saturday Club, whose notables included Ralph Waldo Emerson—whose biography Holmes wrote. Other works by him are *Homeopathy and Its Kindred Delusions* and a paper on "The Contagiousness of Puerperal Fever" detailing his major medical discovery.

Holmes was dean of the Harvard Medical School as well as a longtime professor of anatomy. His father, who wrote the first history of the town of Cambridge, was beloved pastor of the First Parish and First Church of Cambridge until the Unitarian controversy arose. His son, Oliver Wendell Holmes, Jr., was a distinguished member of the Supreme Court of the United States.

LOUISA MAY ALCOTT

1832-1888

Courtesy of the sculptor, Daniel Altshuler

The author of *Little Women* was educated at home by her father, Amos Bronson Alcott, founder of the innovative Temple School in Concord as well as of the Fruitlands utopian community in Harvard, Massachusetts—both of which quickly failed. Bronson was never able to provide adequately for his wife and daughter through his traveling lectures on Transcendental philosophy, so young Louisa did varied available work to help support the family. Her interest in writing led to a publisher's suggestion that she write a book for girls. This autobiographical book about her family was an immediate bestseller.

Louisa had access to the library of Ralph Waldo Emerson and was acquainted with Margaret Fuller. As her family's breadwinner, she wrote hundreds of articles and books, both popular fiction and nonfiction. She produced almost one book per year, including *Hospital Sketches*, reporting on her experience as a Civil War nurse. She contracted typhoid fever and suffered continuing ill health and exhaustion. When her father was dying in Boston, she visited despite her weakness and died just two days after his death. At age fifty-five she was buried beside her parents in Concord's Sleepy Hollow.

NATHANIEL HAWTHORNE

1804-1864

Courtesy of the Library of Congress

While struggling to become a self-supporting writer, Hawthorne accepted an American magazine position promising $500 per year. After six issues, the publisher declared bankruptcy and provided only $20. Income from a job measuring salt and coal in the Boston Custom House was invested in the Brook Farm utopia, which also failed, as narrated in *The Blithedale Romance*.

After the successful publication of *Twice-Told Tales*, Hawthorne married Sophia Amelia Peabody and moved to Concord, where their friends included Ralph Waldo Emerson, Henry David Thoreau, and Margaret Fuller.

After three distracting years working as a surveyor of the Salem Custom House and the disturbing death of his mother, he was prodded to write his probing first novel, *The Scarlet Letter*, portraying a proud adulteress condemned to wear a scarlet "A" on her dress. Herman Melville dedicated *Moby Dick* to Nathaniel Hawthorne, thereby publicly recognizing his genius.

A college friend, President Franklin Pierce—whose political biography Hawthorne had written—appointed him consul to Liverpool, England. Upon returning home to Concord seven years later, his health deteriorated. He was buried in 1864 in the Sleepy Hollow Cemetery.

JAMES T. FIELDS

1817-1881

Courtesy of Coe College

At seventeen, Fields traveled from his home in Portsmouth, New Hampshire, to Boston, where he apprenticed at the Old Corner Bookstore and began writing for newspapers. After he was invited to join a major publishing firm, it soon became known as Ticknor and Fields; now, James T. Fields is celebrated in *American National Biography* as the foremost publisher of literature in mid-nineteenth century America. He succeeded James Russell Lowell as editor of the *Atlantic Monthly*.

Fields not only published eminent authors but frequently established intimate relations with them. Among his contacts in English literature were Charles Dickens, George Eliot, Alfred Tennyson, and Thomas De Quincy. American authors of his acquaintance included Hawthorne, Holmes, Emerson, Whittier, Harriet Beecher Stowe, and Bret Harte, whom he brought East from California.

HERMAN MELVILLE

1819-1891

Courtesy of the Library of Congress

In the prologue to his biography of Herman Melville, Lewis Mumford states that Melville shares with Walt Whitman the distinction of being the greatest imaginative writer America has produced. He says that in depth of religious insight there is no one in the nineteenth century to compare with him except Dostoyevsky.

Herman was born in New York City of Scottish-Dutch ancestors. One of his grandfathers joined the Boston Tea Party of 1773. A series of misfortunes, beginning with his father's early death, preceded his shipping out on the whaler "Acushnet." He jumped ship in Polynesia, a story he immortalized in *Typee* in 1848. This early work remained in print throughout his lifetime and was distributed worldwide thanks partly to its erotic symbolism.

Despite financial difficulties, he continued to write, with high encouragement from his friend Nathaniel Hawthorne. Melville's masterpiece, *Moby-Dick*, was the story of a whaling expedition and initially received small praise and small sales. He spent years in rheumatic pain, writing short stories for magazines, until he was relieved by his appointment as an inspector of customs in New York City, where he joined the All Souls Unitarian Church.

When he died, there was only one obituary notice, which contained only four lines. Not until the 1950s did Herman Melville find recognition for what the *Encyclopaedia Britannica* names a novel not equaled in scope by any previous piece of American literature and never matched in its portentous portrayal of human struggle with the forces of the universe.

GEORGE W. CURTIS

1824-1892

Courtesy of the Special Collections Library of the Pennsylvania State University

Curtis's father was a United States senator and the chief justice of Rhode Island; his mother died when he was two years old. He and his brother were part of the Brook Farm community and school. Curtis later lived in Concord and became acquainted with Emerson, Fuller, and Hawthorne.

On becoming a writer and editor, he wrote the first "Easy Chair" columns for *Harper's New Monthly*. He declined the invitation to be editor of the *New York Times*, but served as chancellor of the University of the State of New York. He spoke on critical issues of the day and authored forty books and pamphlets.

BRET HARTE

1836-1902

John Pettie; oil on canvas 1884;
National Portrait Gallery, Smithsonian Institution

The writer of short stories such as "The Luck of Roaring Camp" grew up in Albany before his family moved to California. He joined the San Francisco Unitarian Church, where Thomas Starr King helped to guide his writing, reading, and concern for the abolition of slavery. When Harte founded a newspaper, *Northern California*, his outraged editorial condemning drunken townsmen who had murdered many Indian women and children forced him to flee for his life.

Harte's writing about California mining camps brought him leadership of a literary group that included Mark Twain and Ambrose Bierce. Upon moving to Boston, he was celebrated by Emerson, Lowell, and Longfellow. That peak of success was followed by failure upon failure and deepening debt until President Hayes appointed him to diplomatic posts in Germany and Glasgow.

Volumes of Bret Harte's short fiction were published almost every year during his last twenty years.

Margaret Fuller

1810-1850

Courtesy of the Unitarian Universalist Association

Margaret Fuller grew up in a Unitarian family in Cambridge, and her brother, Arthur, became a Unitarian minister. America's first female correspondent and first book review editor was taught to read at the age of three by her father, Timothy Fuller, a lawyer and U.S. congressman. Although no women were then admitted to Harvard College, Margaret studied with student friends who viewed her as a peer. She was present at the Unitarian Church in Harvard Square when Emerson delivered his famous address on "The American Scholar." Later, he and his wife invited her to live in their Concord home. Fuller and Emerson jointly founded a Transcendentalist journal, *The Dial*, first edited by her and then by him.

Her educational "Conversations" for prominent Boston women concerning issues central in their lives was followed by her becoming the editor of the *New York Daily Tribune* and the author of *Women in the Nineteenth Century*. As the *Tribune's* foreign correspondent reporting on European cities, she journeyed to Rome and met a son of Italian aristocrats, Angelo Ossoli, who was fighting with the exiled patriot, Mazzini. When Rome fell, she, Ossoli, and their son chose to sail to America. Their ship sank in a storm just four hundred yards away from New York City. All three drowned.

A plaque at the Margaret Fuller Memorial in Cambridge honors her as "a teacher, writer, critic of literature and art, a companion and helper of many reformers in America and Europe."

WILLIAM WARE

1797-1852

*Courtesy of the University of
Viriginia Collections, Charlottesville*

The first Unitarian minister in New York City served from 1821 to 1836. Upon resigning, he bought—and served as editor of—the *Christian Examiner*. Three dramatic novels by him—*Zenobia, Probus,* and *Julian*—were set in early Christian times and were popular. His fictional narrative of the life of Christ was the first widely read American religious novel.

William was a son of Henry Ware, Sr., of Harvard University. He suffered ill health, with disturbing occasions of epilepsy. Nevertheless, he proceeded with his work as writer and editor, producing *Sketches of European Capitals, American Unitarian Biography,* and a volume celebrating the genius of Washington Allston, painter of "Belshazzar's Feast."

Richard Hildreth

1807-1865

Courtesy of the Unitarian Universalist Association

Born in Deerfield, Massachusetts, Hildreth is remembered as a journalist and author, whose father, Hosea Hildreth, became a Unitarian minister after he was disowned by Congregationalists when he persistently exchanged pulpits with Unitarian ministers.

He became a principle editor of the *New York Tribune* after he wrote America's first antislavery novel—*The Slave: or Memoirs of Archy Moore*—and an antislavery book, *Despotism in America*. In his writing, he emphasized the negative effects of slavery on the South. His wife, Caroline, supported the family for eight years during which he researched and wrote a respected, irreverent story of America's founders entitled *History of the United States of America (1849-1852)*.

LYDIA MARIA FRANCIS CHILD

1802-1880

Courtesy of the Library of Congress

A descendant of Richard Francis (who settled in Cambridge, Massachusetts in 1636), Child was a humanitarian.

She was known as one of America's first women of letters, a reformer and novelist who wrote and edited forty books. Her brother, Convers, was a Unitarian minister who taught at Harvard Divinity School.

Her novel, *Hobomok* (1824), is the first historical novel published in the United States. Her *Appeal in Favor of That Class of Americans Called Africans* (1833) persuaded William Ellery Channing and Charles Sumner to oppose slavery. In 1835 her two-volume *History of the Condition of Women in Various Ages and Nations* voiced her early struggle in this field. She was a founder of the Massachusetts Woman Suffrage Association. Theodore Parker is evident in her three-volume *Progress of Religious Ideas, Through Successive Ages* (1855), which celebrates world religions.

A biography of Mrs. Child by John Greenleaf Whittier is included in *The Letters of Lydia Maria Child* (1882). The poet recited a memorial poem at her funeral. Wendell Phillips delivered the oration.

JOHN FISKE

1842-1901

Courtesy of the Wisconsin State Historical Society

Although at eighteen years of age he declared himself an infidel in opposition to his family's orthodox Congregationalism, John Fiske's devotion to the scientific spirit later led to his affirmation of an evolutionary theism facilitated by Herbert Spencer's philosophy.

Because of his near "atheism," Fiske was not appointed to the Harvard faculty and served, therefore, only as an assistant librarian. In this position, Fiske found ample time for research and writing.

When he was able to do professional lecturing, he gradually grew both popular and wealthy (though he never learned to live within his means). His theme of "American Manifest Destiny" promised a millennium of peace and prosperity.

Having gained a significant amount of weight, Fiske experienced declining health, and died on America's 125th birthday, July 4, 1901.

FRANCIS PARKMAN

1823-1893

Francis Parkman was born in Boston, the son of a Unitarian minister. He studied history at Harvard with President Jared Sparks. Though plagued with illness from childhood on, he was able to travel and write, thanks to a family inheritance.

He and his cousin, Quincy Adams Shaw, traveled from St. Louis along the California and Oregon Trail, camping and hunting with the Sioux Indians and experiencing tribal and frontier life.

Highly esteemed to this day is *The Oregon Trail*, a dramatic narrative of travel before the Gold Rush of 1849. Parkman's nine volumes of realistic and romantic narrative about the conflict between France and England in North America do not exclude atrocities by Native Americans and LaSalle's murder by his own men, who hated his harsh commands.

Frontpiece, "A Life of Francis Parkman," by Charles Haightman

WILLIAM HICKLING PRESCOTT

1796-1859

Courtesy of the Library of Congress

William Prescott was the son of a prominent family, his grandfather having commanded American forces at Bunker Hill. When he was blinded in one eye by a crust of bread flung in the Harvard Commons, he devoted his life to literature. Thanks to ample family means, an assistant was available to read to him. He could remember up to sixty pages while preparing to write chapters of *The History of the Conquest of Mexico* and *The Conquest of Cuba*, both widely read dramatic narratives.

His biography was written by a close Unitarian friend and fellow American historian, George Ticknor.

4. Religion

WILLIAM ELLERY CHANNING

1780-1842

Statue in Touro Park, Newport, Rhode Island
Courtesy of the Channing Memorial Church

When William was thirteen, his father died in Newport, Rhode Island. His mother's father, William Ellery—who had signed the Declaration of Independence—then helped to care for him. When William graduated as class orator, tiny Harvard College was limited to just a few buildings.

Having decided to become a minister, he joined the First Church in Cambridge, which was then served by Dr. Abiel Holmes. When he was twenty-three, in 1803, he was ordained by the Federal Street Church in Boston—now the Arlington Street Church—which he served until his death.

He proclaimed his growing liberalism when he delivered his address on Unitarian Christianity at the ordination of Jared Sparks in Baltimore in 1819. At what has been called the Pentecost of Unitarianism, he articulated a manifesto of the movement of liberal Christians. His rigorous repudiation of the Calvinisitic doctrines of human depravity, predestination, and eternal damnation united with his invigorating affirmation of human freedom, self-culture, and human dignity.

In 1820, he invited colleagues to his parsonage to form an organization uniting liberal clergy. They formed the Berry Street Conference, which led in 1825 to the adoption of a constitution for the American Unitarian Association.

During his lifetime he contributed in notable ways to philosophy, literature, education, and social reform. He is recognized as the primary formative figure in the history of Unitarianism in America.

Jared Sparks

1789-1866

Courtesy of the Unitarian Universalist Association

When Jared Sparks was ordained in Baltimore, Maryland, in 1819, William Ellery Channing delivered a formative historic sermon on "Unitarian Christianity." Sparks was a historian and Unitarian minister who was president of Harvard (1849-1853). He was a pioneer in publishing documents of American History. His works included *The Diplomatic Correspondence of the American Revolution* (twelve volumes), *Works of Benjamin Franklin* (ten volumes), *Works of George Washington*, *Papers of James Madison*, and the *Library of American Biography*.

Theodore Parker

1810-1860

Courtesy of the Unitarian Universalist Association

Theodore Parker's grandfather commanded the Lexington Minutemen on April 19, 1775. Theodore himself battled against holy ignorance and unholy slavery. His 1841 sermon on "The Transient and Permanent in Christianity" resulted in his isolation from most Unitarian colleagues. Some Unitarians of Boston, however, soon made him the most powerful preacher in the city when they organized the Twenty-Eighth Congregational Society of Boston. His radical reforms and applied Transcendentalism were undergirded by his triple affirmation of "God, Duty, and Immortality." Two biographies of his life are *Theodore Parker: Yankee Crusader* by Henry Steele Commager and *American Heretic: Theodore Parker* by Dean Grodzins.

Henry Ware, Sr.

1764-1845

Courtesy of the Unitarian Universalist Association

Henry Ware, Sr. loved to play more than to farm—or to go to school—in Sherborn, Massachusetts, where he was born. However, his classes were limited to six to ten weeks in the winter.

Henry's father died when he was fifteen, so his elder brothers generously pooled their small resources to enable him to attend and to graduate from Harvard College in 1785, the leading scholar of his class.

After preparing for the ministry with Rev. Timothy Hilliard of the First Parish in Cambridge, he was called to Hingham's First Church ("Old Ship") in 1787, serving until 1805, when he was elected to the Hollis Professorship of Divinity in Harvard College. Some of the overseers opposed his election because he was understood to be a Unitarian. When Dr. Jedediah Morse published his opposition, the decision was affirmed by thirty-three to twenty-three.

Professor Ware, despite that early battle with the Calvinists, was so highly esteemed that he twice served as acting president of Harvard.

Henry Ware, Jr.

1794-1843

Courtesy of the Unitarian Universalist Association

This son of the minister/professor who was at the center of the 1805 Unitarian controversy was born in Hingham. He attended Exeter Academy and Harvard College before being voted minister of the Second Church in Boston in 1817.

He married Dr. Benjamin Waterhouse's daughter, Elizabeth. The death of their youngest of three children was followed by his wife's death at the age of thirty in 1824. The next year Ware became one of the founders of the American Unitarian Association and member of its executive committee. When traveling to conduct worship in Northampton, Massachusetts, he experienced a hemorrhage so severe that he was hospitalized in Worcester for six weeks.

Upon recovery of his fragile health, Harvard appointed him professor of pulpit eloquence and pastoral care. Ralph Waldo Emerson, his ministerial colleague at Second Church, became his successor as minister. Dr. Ware's pastoral care expressed his devout relation to a personal God and—despite his continuing respect for Emerson—led him to repudiate Emerson's critique of Christianity.

In 1841, when Dr. Ware was in the pulpit of All Souls Church, New York, his pain required him to dismiss the congregation after the hymn before the sermon. After resigning his Harvard chair in 1841, he died two years later.

AARON BANCROFT

1755-1839

Courtesy of the American Antiquarian Society

Bancroft served for fifty years as minister of the Second Congregational Church (Unitarian) in Worcester, Massachusetts, which was formed after the town voted not to call Bancroft to its First Parish due to his liberal persuasion. Aaron Bancroft held that Jesus Christ was morally heroic but not divine. In 1807, he published his *Life of General Washington*. He served as the first president of the American Unitarian Association. The noted American historian, George Bancroft, was his son.

MARY SAFFORD

1851-1927

Around 1900, a joke was making the rounds in Unitarian circles in Iowa: "What do the Catholics and the Unitarians have in common?" Answer: "They both worship the virgin Mary." Mary Safford was the reason for this joke, as she was nearly worshipped by the Unitarians in Iowa.

Mary Augusta Safford was one of three women from the town of Hamilton, Illinois, who entered the Unitarian ministry and became part of the Iowa Sisterhood. Mary's family moved to Hamilton in 1855. She grew to womanhood under difficult pioneer circumstances, which prepared her for some of the hardships she would encounter later. Although in somewhat fragile health, she was full of life. Her friends said she always cherished those beautiful ideals that make strong men and women.

Although Mary's family strongly objected to her becoming a minister, as well as a Unitarian, she persisted. Under the Reverend Clute's tutelage, she began preaching in Oakwood and in the town hall in Hamilton; she also organized a Unitarian church there in 1878, the first of many she would organize, serve, or revitalize. In 1880, she was ordained at the meeting of the Iowa Unitarian Association in Humboldt, Iowa, and invited to become minister of the Humboldt church, while also serving a small group in Algona. Her friend Eleanor Gordon accompanied her and served as the high school principal in Humboldt in addition to performing many duties in the two churches.

Over the next five years, the Humboldt church was built into a large and successful congregation. Mary and Eleanor moved on to Sioux City, where a group of business people was starting a church. Again, the church was soon in a new building, with a large and enthusiastic congregation and many social, literary, educational, service, and philanthropic activities. Jenkin Lloyd Jones called it "the best pastored church in the West" in 1893. Eleanor left in 1897, and two years later, Mary Safford and her new assistant, Marie Jenney, moved to Des Moines. There, Mary divided her time between the then-struggling Des Moines church and the Iowa Unitarian Association, for which she was field secretary and editor of its publication, *Old & New*. She served as president of the Iowa Unitarian Association for seven years and as field secretary (missionary) for six. She was also a director of the Western Unitarian Conference and the American Unitarian Association.

Throughout her life, Mary Safford was a suffragist. Her approach to this, as well as other social justice issues, was to educate and inspire others so they would become involved, rather than to remain in the spotlight herself (although she did lobby Congress for the Women's Suffrage Amendment). She also served for a time as president of both the Iowa and the Florida Equal Suffrage Associations and was on the board of directors of the National American Suffrage Association.

Mary's death was probably hastened by a serious fall, which fractured her hip and confined her to a wheelchair. Her last public appearance was at the dedication of the high school auditorium in Hamilton, Illinois, which she financed and donated to the town in memory of her mother and all pioneer women. Two weeks later, she died in Orlando. Her body was removed to the home of the Reverend Eleanor Gordon, who had then retired in Hamilton, and a memorial service in her honor was held in the new school auditorium.

Mary left her home in Orlando to the city to be used as an art museum.

By Sarah Oelberg, From *Standing Before US: Unitarian Universalist Women and Social Reform*, edited by Dorothy May Emerson (Boston: Skinner House Books, 2000).

THOMAS STARR KING

1824-1864

Courtesy of the Library of Congress

Mountain peaks were named for this minister, whose eloquent speech and action saved California for the Union during the Civil War.

In the United States Capitol stands a statue of Starr King as a citizen symbolizing the people of California. A similar statue stands in the Golden Gate Park.

This son of a Universalist minister (who died when Starr was fifteen) had to work to support his family. Intense self-education, united with the encouragement and social support of Theodore Parker and Henry Whitney Bellows, preceded his call to the pulpit of the Hollis Street Unitarian Church in Boston. Following his service in Boston, from 1848 to 1860, Starr King became minister of the Unitarian Church of San Francisco. His sermons and lectures attracted huge audiences and gained him the award of an honorary degree from Harvard University.

One cryptic sentence attributed to Starr King is: "The Universalists think God is too good to damn them forever; the Unitarians think they are too good to be damned forever."

EDWARD EVERETT HALE

1822-1909

Courtesy of the Library of Congress

In his latter years, this Unitarian minister—who was esteemed as both an author and reformer—was unanimously elected chaplain of the United States Senate. Hale was personally acquainted with Dolly Madison, John Quincy Adams, Theodore Roosevelt, and William Howard Taft—not to mention Emerson, Lowell, Webster, Holmes, and Julia Ward Howe.

Hale's uncle was the orator and statesman, Edward Everett. His father owned and edited Boston's *Daily Advertiser*. Hale began his career as a legislative reporter, ultimately writing and editing sixty books. Most popular was his 1863 tale, *A Man Without a Country*, about a traitor who said in court that he wished he might never hear of the United States again. Accordingly, the man was banished to sea, forced to live aboard boats for more than fifty-six years.

Educated at Harvard, Edward Everett Hale began his Unitarian ministry by serving for ten years in Worcester, Massachusetts, and then for forty-three years pastoring Boston's South Congregational Church (Unitarian). He was keen to abolish slavery, advance tolerance, and reform public education, as well as to have the government regulate monopolies.

Asked when he was a U.S. Senate chaplain, "Do you pray for the senators, Dr. Hale?" he replied, "No, I look at the senators, and pray for the country."

JOHN PIERPONT

1785-1866

Courtesy of Old Sturbridge Village

Upon graduating from Yale in 1804, John Pierpont became a tutor in South Carolina and the author of two successful school readers. As a Unitarian abolitionist, he became minister of the prestigious Hollis Street Church in Boston for twenty-five years, until a few persistent parishioners—who were wealthy pro-slavery rum merchants—forced his resignation in 1845. Later, he served as minister in Troy, New York, and Medford, Massachusetts.

A granite marker in Mount Auburn Cemetery, Cambridge, celebrates his life as "Poet, Preacher, Philosopher, Philanthropist." John Pierpont's grandson was J. P. Morgan, the powerful financier of industrial America.

JAMES FREEMAN CLARKE

1810-1888

Courtesy of the Unitarian Universalist Association

After graduating from Harvard College and Harvard Divinity School, Clarke served in Louisville, Kentucky, where he established the *Western Messenger*, a periodical of the Transcendentalist movement.

Moving to Boston, he founded the Church of the Disciples in 1841 and was one of the few ministers to exchange pulpits with Theodore Parker. After a serious health crisis in 1849, he resumed his Boston ministry for thirty-four more years.

Clarke proclaimed five points of Unitarian faith:

1. The Fatherhood of God
2. The Brotherhood of Man
3. The Leadership of Jesus
4. Salvation by Character
5. The Progress of Mankind, onward and upward forever.

In contrast to the Transcendentalists and the Free Religious Association, Clarke united with Frederic Henry Hedge and Henry W. Bellows in a "Broad Church" movement committed to unified Unitarian church organization and action.

One of his books, *Ten Great Religions,* is an early comparative study of world religions.

CHARLES FOLLEN

1795-1840

Photomontage by Bartek Malysa. Portrait courtesy of Harvard University.

Born the son of a counselor-at-law and judge in Germany, Follen was in 1818 awarded a Doctor of Civil Law degree and was appointed to a lectureship on jurisprudence at the University of Giessen in Germany.

He was suspected, though never convicted, of intrigue when a fanatical friend assassinated a Russophile diplomat. Facing possible imprisonment, he escaped to Switzerland before fleeing to the United States in 1824. Letters of introduction by General Lafayette helped his acceptance in Boston.

In 1828, he married Eliza Lee Cabot, daughter of Samuel and Sarah Cabot of Boston. In 1829, Follen taught German at Harvard and wrote a *German Reader for Beginners* and a *German Grammar*. He introduced the first gymnasium equipment to Harvard University. He was appointed as a professor in 1830, but was not reappointed in 1835, partly due to his antislavery agitation.

He introduced a decorated Christmas tree—a custom now widespread across the continent.

In 1836, with the assistance of William Ellery Channing, he was ordained a Unitarian minister and served a new congregation in East Lexington where the octagonal church building he designed, known as the Follen Church, still stands.

On return from delivering a lecture in New York, he embarked on the steamer *Lexington*, which caught fire while at sea. Follen, along with other passengers, perished in the tragedy.

A five-volume set of his papers and his biography was prepared by his wife.

Book from the collection of historical textbooks in the Special Collections, Monroe C. Gutman Library, Harvard Graduate School of Education. Gymnastics engravings from Turnbuch für die Söhne Vaterlandes (1817), by J.C.F. Gutsmuth, courtesy of Harvard College Library.

Frederic Henry Hedge

1805-1890

Courtesy of the Unitarian Universalist Association

Frederic was educated mainly by his father, Levi Hedge, Harvard's Alford Professor of Natural Religion, Moral Philosophy, and Civil Polity. At the age of thirteen, accompanied by his tutor, George Bancroft (who would later become a distinguished American historian), Hedge studied in Europe for four years before entering Harvard College and the Divinity School. Ordained in West Cambridge (now Arlington), Massachusetts, Hedge counted Emerson and Margaret Fuller among his friends. Although he wrote the very first article describing the Transcendentalist movement and also organized the Transcendentalist Club—which initiated the Transcendentalist periodical, *The Dial*—he emphasized the ideal of the Christian Church existing through the generations.

In addition to his parish work in West Cambridge and Bangor, Maine, he taught the history of the Christian Church, as well as German language and literature, at Harvard.

Among his major publications are *Prose Writers of Germany* and *Reason in Religion*.

Hedge's most popular literary piece, still shared across the centuries, is his translation of Martin Luther's hymn, "A Mighty Fortress is Our God."

ANDREW PRESTON PEABODY

1811-1893

A Unitarian minister and writer, Peabody was Plummer Professor of Christian Morals and preacher to Harvard University from 1860 to 1881; he would also twice serve as acting president.

A bronze table in the Memorial Church declares that for thirty-three years, Andrew Preston Peabody "moved among the teachers and students of Harvard College, and wist not that his face shone."

His 1875 address—delivered on the Cambridge Common in celebration of George Washington's acceptance of command of the Continental Army—stated:

> Cambridge was the first capital of the infant republic. By adopting the army, and choosing its head, the colonies performed their first act, not of alliance, but of organic unity, and became a nation unawares.
>
> Year after year, on the commencement platform in the old parish-church, had successive ranks of earnest young men rehearsed to greedy ears the dream of liberty which they pledged faith and life to realize.

Washington remained in the Vassall House, now Mr. Longfellow's, until the following April. He generally attended worship at the church of the First Parish.

HENRY WHITNEY BELLOWS

1814-1882

Courtesy of the Unitarian Universalist Association

The Bellows family home was an ancestral farm in New Hampshire, close to Bellows Falls on the Connecticut River in Vermont. Here, Henry grew up without a mother, for she died when he was two years old.

Following his education at Harvard College and Divinity School, he served from 1837 until his death as the pastor of the First Unitarian Church of New York, now named the Unitarian Church of All Souls.

Dr. Bellows was a principal founder of the Century Club, the Union League, and the Harvard Club of New York. His committee work was extensive through the Civil War era. Bellows was the founder and president the United States Sanitary Commission during and after the war. This commission later merged with the International Red Cross.

In addition to being the first president of the New York Civil Service Association, he poured his energy into the formation of the National Conference of Unitarian and Other Christian Churches. His institutional churchmanship reflected his disenchantment with Emersonian tendencies toward "thin, ghostly individualism and meager congregationalism."

ROBERT COLLYER

1823-1912

Courtesy of the Unitarian Universalist Association

Both of Collyer's parents in England were orphans who worked in the same mill. He had only a few months of school. At fourteen he became a blacksmith, a job he held for twelve years. When his wife died in childbirth, he gained strength by becoming a Methodist and soon thereafter a volunteer preacher of power.

He and his new wife sailed for America, where he found employment outside Philadelphia making claw hammers. Upon listening to Lucretia Mott, he joined the abolitionist cause and thereby met William Henry Furness, who invited him to speak from his Unitarian pulpit. The Methodists then staged a trial, related to his lack of support for Methodist dogmas (and encouraged by his growing abolitionist convictions). Since the lay preacher could not answer their questions, he resigned.

Dr. Furness recommended that the former blacksmith serve as a much-needed Unitarian minister-at-large in Chicago, where Robert Collyer proved a popular preacher and lyceum platform speaker. Chicago's North Church congregation built a new church. It turned to ashes in the Great Fire of 1871, which also destroyed their home and his library. After total immersion in relief work and construction of a new church, he was invited in 1874 to serve the Church of the

Messiah in New York. He declined. Upon repetition of the offer five years later, he accepted and served a flourishing congregation, finally being succeeded in 1907 by John Haynes Holmes, whose first book was *The Life and Letters of Robert Collyer.*

JENKIN LLOYD JONES

1843-1918

Jones's boyhood was spent on a Wisconsin farm, and, after service in the Civil War, he had to struggle hard to work his way through Meadville Theological School. As pastor at Janesville, Wisconsin, he developed an involvement with the Western Unitarian Conference (WUC), becoming its secretary in 1875 and a full-time missionary secretary in 1880. From that position he led western Unitarianism in a radical direction, founding the periodical *Unity* to help foster his efforts.

Jenkin Lloyd Jones was the leader of the Unity Men, the radically modernist element in Midwest Unitarianism of the later nineteenth century. Jones had a forceful personality and was a tireless worker; he combined these traits to lead the Western Unitarian Conference on a largely independent path from Boston Unitarianism. He stressed an absolutely creedless "ethical basis" as the common element in the churches he wanted to bring together, a theological position that left Christology—and some believed even theology—in the background. He was also a pioneer in religious education, embodying his liberal views in Sunday-school work.

Although Jones was the most powerful Western figure in the denomination, he encountered friction from the

American Unitarian Association (AUA) because of his independent course, and from within the WUC because of his theological radicalism. In 1882, Jones reorganized the Fourth Unitarian Society in Chicago as All Souls Church, and a decade later he played a central role in the World's Parliament of Religions, which brought together a number of world religious leaders. The conference seemed a step toward Jones's dream of a universal church for humankind. He ended his career as director of the Abraham Lincoln Centre in Chicago, where he continued to be a voice of reform. In his last years, he spoke as a pacifist in opposition to World War I.

From *The Unitarians and the Universalists* by David Robinson (Westport CT: Greenwood Press, 1985)

SAMUEL McCHORD CROTHERS

1857-1927

Courtesy of the First Parish in Cambridge

Samuel McChord Crothers was well known in his own days as the author of familiar essays—often appearing in the *Atlantic Monthly*—in which he treated human foibles with a gentle, humorous touch. His parishioners saw another side of him: the religious thinker who knew how to take old dogmas and discover what of value still remained in them; a preacher of singular elevation of thought; the leader of a congregation who encouraged his people in social welfare projects so subtly, that they hardly knew what had moved them; the pastor "who, when a mother was dead, said oh, so very little, but just the right thing."

Of him, Francis Greenwood Peabody wrote: "When we try to sum up the character that lay behind this lofty teaching, is not the word which comes most easily to our lips the word serenity? This habitual serenity gave him a singular degree of moral courage in decisions of causes and minorities, especially when they were unpopular or undefended; and he brought to their defense, not the fearlessness of a fighter, but the higher courage of a completely tranquil and confident friend." No minister in the history of the church more completely won the trust and affection of his congregation.

EZRA STILES GANNETT

1801-1871

Courtesy of the Unitarian Universalist Association

Ezra Gannett was born in Cambridge, Massachusetts. His mother, Ruth Stiles—daughter of the president of Yale—died when he was seven. When he graduated from Harvard College and Divinity School, William Ellery Channing knocked on his door, whereupon he became Channing's colleague and eventual successor. He was minister when the church moved from Federal Street to Arlington Street, opposite the Public Garden. Gannett was an excellent extemporaneous Unitarian preacher in this commanding post.

An organizer, Gannett not only fostered the Unitarian Association, but also its administrative officer function. He supported the association's ministry-at-large to the Boston poor. However, after twelve exhausting years, he escaped to Europe for two years of recovery. Soon after his return, a paralytic stroke left him a cripple who now required the adept use of two canes to walk. Despite his limp, he preached, co-edited the *Christian Examiner*, and opposed the Transcendentalist emphasis on immediate inspiration and the immanence of God affirmed by Emerson and Parker. Harvard named him a Doctor of Divinity.

Although Ezra Gannett hated slavery, he prayed, "God save us from disunion!"

ANTOINETTE BROWN BLACKWELL

1825-1921

Courtesy of the Unitarian Universalist Association

The first woman in America to be ordained (and the first to officiate at a marriage) was born in a log cabin on the family farm near Rochester, New York. At an early age Antoinette was determined to become a minister. With money saved from teaching, she graduated from Oberlin College and was allowed—despite being a woman—to study theology, but she was not allowed to graduate.

She then lectured on women's rights, temperance, and anti-slavery issues. Thomas Wentworth Higginson and Theodore Parker invited her to preach in their Unitarian churches.

In 1856, Antoinette Brown was ordained and installed in the Congregational Church in South Butler, New York. Upon marrying abolitionist and suffragist Samuel Blackwell, she became a Unitarian and helped to found All Souls Unitarian Church in Elizabeth, New Jersey, later being elected minister *emerita*.

At the World's Congress of Religion she declared, "Women have become indispensable to the religious evolution of the human race."

Oberlin College awarded her the degree of Doctor of Divinity. She died in 1921 at the age of ninety-six.

OCTAVIUS BROOKS FROTHINGHAM

1822-1895

Courtesy of the Unitarian Universalist Association

Upon graduating from Harvard College and Divinity School, this son of the minister of the First Church in Boston was ordained at the North Church in Salem in 1847. His decision to resign in 1855 was triggered by the reenslavement of Anthony Burns under the Fugitive Slave Act. Attacking Christianity for its complicity with slavery, he refused to administer communion.

When minister of the Independent Liberal Church of New York in 1859, he gathered a large congregation of hearers. When a little group of radicals formed the Free Religious Association, they persuaded him to be president to lend visibility and weight to their undertaking.

Frothingham's continuing career as a biographer and historian brought forth major works such as: *The Religion of Humanity, Theodore Parker, Transcendentalism in New England,* and *Boston Unitarianism: 1820-1850.*

Upon returning to Boston after retiring, he attended the First Church in Boston (Unitarian), which his father had served.

FRANCIS GREENWOOD PEABODY

1847-1936

Courtesy of the Andover-Harvard Theological Library

After serving for five years as the minister of the First Church (Unitarian) in Harvard Square, Peabody taught college and theological students Christian ethics at Harvard, specializing in pioneer applications of religion to social problems. Undergraduates described his course as "Peabody's drainage, drunkenness, and divorce." His primary book, *Jesus Christ and the Social Question,* called for social reform rather than a radical reconstruction of society. It emphasized cooperation rather than class conflict. Incidentally, he dared to proclaim, "Jesus Christ came to save men from theologians."

Peabody served for forty years as a trustee of the Hampton Institute, designed to promote the advancement of the American Indian and the American Negro. He was helpful in the founding of the social service and social outreach of college students through the Phillips Brooks House Association.

In order to facilitate his teaching, he introduced the first university department of social ethics and supplemented it by founding the Social Ethics Museum, which featured 6,000 photographs relevant to social reform in America's 1895-1910 period of rapid urbanization, industrialization, and immigration. The photos are now part of Harvard's Fogg Museum. The Museum of Modern Art in New York mounted an exhibition of these candid images of Ellis Island, hospitals, housing, and education in various states in the Midwest as well as the North and the South.

Now standing visibly in appreciation of the life of Francis Greenwood Peabody is the Peabody Terrace along the Charles River, a three-tower complex for married students—one of the most notable designs of Josep Lluis Sert.

CHARLES CARROLL EVERETT

1824-1900

Courtesy of the Andover-Harvard Theological Library

Three years after Charles graduated from Bowdoin College in 1850 he was teaching modern languages there, but when the question of faculty tenure arose, the overseers vetoed the prospect because he was a Unitarian. He then became the minister of the Unitarian Church in Bangor, Maine.

When the minister accepted the Harvard Corporation's invitation to the Bussey Professorship, his courses included "East Asiatic Religions," an innovation in American teaching. When he became dean of the Divinity School, the faculty sought to have each teaching candidate undergo a physical exam. When the dean noted that such a policy might have ruled him out, they withdrew the motion. From youth Dean Everett was blind in one eye.

His publications included *The Science of Thought, Religions Before Christianity*, and *Fichte's Science of Knowledge*.

Francis Greenwood Peabody said of him: "It was permitted to a generation of students for the ministry to be guided and restrained by a character so self-effacing as never to be conspicuous, yet so convincing as to communicate both life and thought."

WILLIAM CHANNING GANNETT

1840-1923

Courtesy of the Rochester Regional Library Council

Born in Boston and christened by William Ellery Channing, William Channing Gannett spent four years helping semi-starved freed slaves in South Carolina before he was ordained and began to serve in the West. He began in then-muddy Milwaukee in 1868, and later served at Unity Church in St. Paul, Minnesota, before moving on to Rochester, New York, where Susan B. Anthony was a member of the congregation. In order to raise the funds required to allow admission of women to the University of Rochester, she pledged her life insurance, while Gannett and his wife, Mary, a birthright Quaker, pledged their house.

He wrote celebratory hymns such as "Bring, O Morn, Thy Music." He facilitated his Unitarian Church and Rochester's Temple Berith Kodesh jointly establishing the Boys Evening Home, where newsboys of all faiths could socialize and learn arts and crafts.

William Channing Gannett was known as a Western radical. Nevertheless, the American Unitarian Association affirmed and distributed his statement of "The Things Most Commonly Believed Today Among Us."

Frank Lloyd Wright wrote *The House Beautiful*, a volume based on an essay by this Unitarian minister.

THOMAS LAMB ELIOT

1841-1936

Courtesy of Special Collections, Eric V. Hauser Library, Reed College

Thomas Lamb Eliot was born in St. Louis, Missouri, on October 13 and died in Portland, Oregon, on April 28, at the age of ninety-four and after sixty-eight years "of selfless service for the public weal." He was the eldest son of Rev. William G. Eliot, D.D., of the Church of the Messiah in St. Louis. Thomas Eliot was a member of the first class (1862) to graduate from Washington University (St. Louis), which his father organized and administered.

After graduation he entered the Harvard Divinity School and graduated in spite of such defective eyesight that it was often necessary to have his books read to him. On November 28, 1865, he married Henrietta Robins Mack of St. Louis. This fortunate and happy union was unbroken for sixty-seven years, and Mrs. Eliot always actively shared her husband's work.

In 1862, Starr King had preached the first liberal sermon in the Northwest. In the summer of 1867, a little chapel was built in Portland. Finally, through the agency of Rev. Charles Lowe of the American Unitarian Association, an invitation was sent to Thomas Eliot to be their minister. Eliot chose the call to the frontier post.

Portland at that time was a remote, pioneer town of some six thousand inhabitants. The streets were deep in mud or dust, according to the weather, and without lights or sidewalks. But the men and women who had settled Portland were prepared to build one of the most stable and orderly communities on the Coast.

Eliot's church became and has always remained strong and influential. From 1872 to 1875 he was County Superintendent of Education. He turned into the church treasury the salary, which he received for his services.

Eliot was never physically vigorous, and after the injury to his eyes, he could not read or write for more than a quarter of an hour without pain. In 1815 he was worn and weary from his pioneer labors. So he resigned, but the church refused to accept his resignation, granting him a year's leave of absence to be spent in Europe. He returned much improved in health, and the money needed for the new church building was in hand.

Dr. Eliot continued as active minister of the church until 1893. His activities were always overflowing into numerous other channels of community service. Indeed, for fifty years there was hardly a movement for civic betterment in which he did not take a leading part. He was president of the Children's Home; of the Oregon Humane Society and of the Portland Associated Charities. He was a director of the Art Association and the Library Association. His church was a fountain of influence and of money for constructive enterprises, and from two of its members—husband and wife—came the endowment of Reed. Eliot was also a member of the board of directors of the American Unitarian Association and a trustee of the Pacific Unitarian School at Berkeley.

Few ministers have had so honorable a career. He was, in truth, "a citizen minister." He saw the city of his adoption grow from a small frontier town to a handsome, well-ordered city of more than three hundred thousand people, and no other single individual contributed so much as he to the higher life of the community. The Eliot glacier on Mt. Hood is named for him.

In 1889 Harvard gave him the honorary degree of Doctor of Divinity in absentia; in 1912 Washington University made him an honorary Doctor of Laws; and Reed College conferred on him the degree of Doctor of Letters.

Henry Wilder Foote, abridged from Heralds of a Liberal Faith, Volume IV, edited by Samuel Atkins Eliot.

SAMUEL ATKINS ELIOT

1862-1950

Courtesy of Michael McGiffert

The son of Charles W. Eliot—who, as president of Harvard University, decisively shaped higher education in the United States—Samuel provided a somewhat comparable vision and administrative ability with respect to the development of the American Unitarian Association.

An illustrated biography of Eliot is available online as part of Harvard Square Library's Notable American Unitarians, 1936–1961.

5. Social Change

ELIZABETH CADY STANTON

1881-1902

Courtesy of the National Portrait Gallery, Smithsonian Institution

The foremost advocate of women's rights in the nineteenth century was the daughter of a Johnston, New York, lawyer and congressman. In 1840, Elizabeth Cady married an antislavery orator, Henry Stanton. They had seven children.

In 1848 at Seneca Falls, New York, she formulated the first organized demand for women's suffrage in the United States. A New York statute based on her petitions granted property rights to married women. With Lucretia Mott, she led the first women's rights convention in the United States and drafted its Declaration of Sentiments demanding that government of women without their consent must end.

In 1856, Elizabeth Cady Stanton met Susan B. Anthony. They united to create a movement for women's rights that transformed social relations in America.

After the Civil War she toured the nation, speaking as the president of the National Woman Suffrage Association.

In 1876, she and Matilda Gage wrote the *Woman's Declaration of Rights*, which Susan B. Anthony presented at the Philadelphia Exposition.

Between 1881 and 1885 came the first three volumes of the *History of Woman Suffrage*, coauthored by Anthony, Gage, and Stanton.

In 1895 her *Woman's Bible* revealed organized religion's idolatry—its devotion to a book consistently fostering male domination and the subordination of women.

A statue of Elizabeth Cady Stanton, Lucretia Mott, and Susan B. Anthony now stands in the United States Capitol.

Susan B. Anthony

1820-1906

Courtesy of the National Portrait Gallery, Smithsonian Insitution

After her father lost his management position when the town's cotton mill collapsed in the panic of 1837, Susan taught school for ten years and then ran her father's farm near Rochester. In 1851, she met Elizabeth Cady Stanton, with whom she labored for the rest of her life to win women's rights, including the right to vote. While Stanton had responsibilities as a mother, Anthony traveled ceaselessly. Together they founded the Women's National League, which gathered and presented to Congress, through Senator Charles Sumner, petitions with 400,000 signatures for the abolition of slavery.

Together, Anthony and Stanton founded the National Women's Suffrage Association (NWSA) in 1869. When Anthony joined a group to vote in Rochester in 1872, she was arrested and sentenced, but she refused to pay the fine. When she died, she left a legacy symbolized by the fact that women suffragists celebrate the Nineteenth Amendment to the Constitution of the United States as the Susan B. Anthony Amendment.

JULIA WARD HOWE

1819-1910

Courtesy of the National Portrait Gallery, Smithsonian Institution

Julia Ward Howe, born in New York City, was the daughter of a Wall Street broker and banker and of a mother who was a poet. Her mother died when she was five. She was educated by governesses and at young ladies' schools.

Julia had published essays on Goethe and Schiller before she married Samuel Gridley Howe, who was affiliated with the Perkins School for the Blind in Boston. Although they had six children, the marriage was tempestuous. He opposed her having any public role and also resented her having a legacy of $3,000 per year.

Julia Ward Howe was a friend of the prophetic preacher Theodore Parker. During the Civil War, her poem, "The Battle Hymn of the Republic," appeared in the *Atlantic Monthly*. It was an instant hit when sung to the tune of "John Brown's Body."

The embattled President Lincoln wept when he first heard it sung.

Julia Ward Howe became a transformer of culture. She was the co-leader, with Lucy Stone, of the American Woman Suffrage Association; served as president of the American Association for Women; and helped to found the General Federation of Women's Clubs.

She was the founder of the weekly *Woman's Journal*, and contributed for twenty years to its encouragement of coeducation, as well as its advocacy of legal, racial, and gender equality. She wrote a biography of Margaret Fuller. She was also the first woman elected to the American Academy of Arts and Letters.

Julia Ward Howe was a Unitarian who sometimes preached from the pulpit of Boston's esteemed Church of the Disciples, of which she was a member.

At her last party, before she died at the age of ninety-one, she insisted on sampling the champagne.

Only 4,000 people could be admitted to the memorial service honoring her, which was held in Boston's Symphony Hall.

LUCY STONE

1818-1893

Courtesy of the Library of Congress

An ancestor of Lucy Stone arrived in Massachusetts in 1635, and one of her grandfathers was a captain in the American Revolution. She grew up in a farm family. When sixteen, she taught school before attending Oberlin College in Ohio—a coeducational college opposed to slavery.

When Lucy Stone was appointed an Anti-Slavery Society lecturer, she agreed to speak for them only on weekends. This meant she was free to lecture weekdays on women's rights. She declared, "I was a woman before I was an abolitionist. I must speak for the women."

Upon accepting Unitarianism, she was expelled from her Congregational church.

When she married, she kept her own name: Mrs. Stone.

When she refused to pay taxes to a government in which she could not participate, household goods were seized.

Mrs. Stone was a founder of the American Equal Rights Association, which worked for voting rights irrespective of race and sex. Her influence was especially effective throughout the forty-seven years she edited *Woman's Journal*, with assistance from her husband, Henry Blackwell, and their daughter, Alice Stone Blackwell.

When she died, she was the first person to be cremated in New England.

JOSEPH TUCKERMAN

1778-1840

Courtesy of the Unitarian Universalist Association

Joseph's father, Edward Tuckerman, though a man of modest means, was a close friend of a statesman of the American Revolution, John Hancock. Joseph was a Harvard College classmate and friend of William Ellery Channing.

He accepted the call to be pastor of the farming village of Chelsea outside Boston. His wife, Abigail Parkman, mother of their three children, died four years later. Aside from his ministry to all the families in town, he provided special assistance to seamen. In 1924, Harvard College honored him as a Doctor of Divinity.

After serving in Chelsea for twenty-five years, he devoted the rest of his life to a pioneering urban ministry-at-large, serving the poor in the city of Boston with support from the American Unitarian Association. The Benevolent Fraternity of Churches was formed in 1834 to carry on such work, which is now named the Unitarian Universalist Urban Ministry.

Dr. Tuckerman's action to advance urban social work and social action inspired community service in other towns and cities. In the early twenty-first century, there are a rapidly growing number of Unitarian Universalist clergy in community ministry rather than in parish ministry or ministry of religious education.

JOSEPHINE SHAW LOWELL

1843-1905

Unsentimental Reformer: The Life of Josephine Shaw Lowell by Joan Waugh, published by Harvard University Press in 1999, celebrates the sister of Colonel Robert Gould Shaw. Josephine's husband, Charles Russell Lowell, Jr., died a hero in battle, never seeing their daughter Carlotta, who died one month before his death.

His widow, who wore black for the rest of her life, went back to the family on Staten Island, where she had been married in the Unitarian Church. Her lifelong Unitarian faith was decisively manifest in her career of fostering organized philanthropy and government service. She began her day-and-night labor helping to establish schools for black children in the South. On being appointed by Governor Tilden, she became the first woman commissioner of the New York State Board of Charities, lobbying and legislating on behalf of the poor.

Her biographer says that a belief in a just and human God permeated her work of national urban reform, the unionization of labor, and being a leader of the Anti-Imperialist League of New York, opposing both the Spanish-American and Philippine-American Wars. Though she suffered attacks and condemnation, she became the founder of the New York City's Charity Organization Society and was a national exemplar and interpreter of the social reform movement nationwide.

Public recognition of her achievement came shortly after her death. The Fountain Terrace of Bryant Park of the New York Public Library displays the pink granite Josephine Shaw Lowell Fountain, the city's first public memorial dedicated to a woman.

EDWIN D. MEAD

1849-1937

Edwin Doak Mead—reformer, editor, and author—was a direct descendant of Gabriel Mead, who settled in Dorchester, Massachusetts, in 1635. Edwin worked on his father's cattle farm and attended local school until the age of thirteen. A studious boy, he married a sister of John Humphrey Noyes, the communitarian socialist. Before becoming a Yankee reformer, he studied at the British Museum and the universities of Cambridge, Oxford, and Leipzig.

In 1890, Edward Everett Hale bequeathed the *New England Magazine*—which they had jointly founded in 1889—to Mead. Mead's work helped to lay the groundwork for the Progressive Era. He was the president of the Free Religious Association and the Men's Woman's Suffrage League. He directed the historical work of Boston's Old South Church, including the editing and publishing of a long influential series of classic documents of the American experience called *Old South Leaflets*.

SAMUEL GRIDLEY HOWE

1801-1876

Courtesy of Perkins School for the Blind

In 1825, after graduating from Harvard Medical School, Dr. Howe participated in the Greek war for independence. He also wrote a sketch of the Greek Revolution. Because he was seeking a new profession, he visited Europe in order to learn how to educate blind children. He taught Laura Bridgman—who had been blind and deaf since age two—how to communicate. The Perkins School for the Blind, a pioneer institution in the United States (which he founded), was awarded both private and government funding, and his action also led to public education and improved treatments for mentally handicapped children.

He and his wife, Julia Ward Howe, jointly edited an antislavery paper, and she wrote the Civil War "Battle Hymn of the Republic."

HENRY BERGH

1811-1888

Courtesy of the Wisconsin Humane Society

Born in New York City, Henry and a brother ran their retired father's shipbuilding company. When President Lincoln appointed Henry Bergh secretary of the American Legation in Russia, he was horrified to see animals treated cruelly. A visit in London to the Royal Society for the Prevention of Cruelty to Animals awakened his decisive action to secure a charter not only to incorporate the American Society for the Prevention of Cruelty to Animals, but also to exercise the power to arrest and prosecute violators of the law. Local governments across the United States and Canada formed similar societies affirming: Animals have rights! Animal beatings and cockfights are illegal! Sick or injured horses can no longer be left to die on the streets!

In 1874, an incident of abuse of a child named Mary Ellen led people to join with Bergh in establishing the New York Society for the Prevention of Cruelty to Children.

DOROTHEA DIX

1802-1887

From a daguerrotype, about 1840

Dorothea Lynde Dix was born in Maine, where she taught school before moving to Boston and opening her own school. Her students included the daughters of William Ellery Channing. When Dorothea contracted tuberculosis, her close friend, William Ellery Channing, aided her recuperation, during which time she produced several books for publication.

After recovering her health, she received an inheritance large enough to free her from teaching. She visited a jail, where she saw mentally ill women prisoner in dirty, cold cells. Her visits with three Unitarian reformers–Horace Mann, Charles Sumner, and Samuel Gridley Howe–led her to investigate what was happening to ill and imprisoned people in some 500 towns. Her 1843 documentary *Memorial to the Massachusetts Legislature* awakened relief, which led her to campaign in other states. After visiting state penitentiaries, county jails, and poorhouses in the Midwest, the South, and Canada, she lobbied legislators there and in Washington, D.C. She proposed that federal land-grant of 12,500,000 acres be set aside as a public endowment to benefit the deaf, mute, and insane. The U.S. Senate and House passed her recommendation by two-thirds. President Franklin Pierce vetoed it.

Dorothea was more successful with Queen Victoria and Parliament when she visited Scotland. Next came a year of visits to the nations of Central Europe. Upon her return home, funds finally began to be allocated for the mentally ill. During the Civil War, she was appointed superintendent of U.S. Army Nurses.

Samuel J. May

1797-1871

Courtesy of the First Parish in Norwell, Massachusetts

An antislavery Unitarian minister—he aided traveling slaves in their journeys northward to Canada—May was the first clergyman to advocate female suffrage. An ally of Parker, Emerson, and Mann, he was the first president of America's pioneering Normal School for Women in Lexington, Massachusetts. He ministered in Syracuse at what is now named the May Memorial Church. When he died, Andrew D. White, then president of Cornell University, spoke of him as "the best man, the most truly Christian man, I have ever known."

Charles Henry Appleton Dall

1816-1886

Courtesy of the Unitarian Universalist Association

Born in Baltimore, Dall attended Harvard Divinity School after graduating in 1840 from Harvard College, along with Henry David Thoreau. After serving as a minister-at-large in St. Louis, Baltimore, and Portsmouth, New Hampshire, he became "the first and only American Unitarian foreign missionary."

Dall ministered on behalf of the American Unitarian Association in Calcutta, India, from 1855 until his death in 1886. His work with Hindu social and religious reformers Ram Mohan Roy and Keshab Chandra Sen, led to their joining Unitarianism and his joining the Brahmo Somaj Hindu society. American and Indian traditions were mutually affirmed. This historic period has been termed the Bengal Renaissance of the nineteenth century. See *Unitarians in India* by Spencer Lavan (Boston: Beacon Press, 1977).

JABEZ T. SUNDERLAND

1842-1936

Courtesy of the Unitarian Universalist Association

This American Unitarian minister was born in England and went on to launch the first major indictment of British imperialism in India. His attack appeared in 1908 in an *Atlantic Monthly* magazine article disclosing "The New Nationalistic Movement in India." Sunderland declared: "India is a subject land. She is a dependent of Great Britain, not a colony. Britain's free colonies are really self-ruling in everything except their relations with foreign powers. Not so with dependencies like India. They are ruled absolutely by Great Britain, which is not their 'mother' country but their conqueror and master."

His book *India in Bondage* was suppressed in India but hailed in America by *Time* magazine.

Jabez Sunderland was the first American to participate in the new Indian National Congress.

Sunderland's two journeys to India encouraged an alliance between the British and American Unitarian associations and the Brahmo Samaj religious and social reform Hindu movement in India.

From the Ann Arbor Unitarian Church in Michigan, he led the battle for advanced nondogmatic theism against nontheism. When he died in Ann Arbor, his memorial service held at the Community Church of New York celebrated his role in liberating India and his promotion of liberating religion in North America.

6. Education

NINE UNITARIAN PRESIDENTS OF HARVARD

1810-1933

This is the only known photograph of five Harvard Presidents together. From left to right, Josiah Quincy (1829-1845), Edward Everett (1846-1849), Jared Sparks (1849-1853), James Walker (1853-1860), and Cornelius Conway Felton (1860-1862).

In continuous service were nine presidents from 1810 to 1933, including John T. Kirkland, Thomas Hill, Charles W. Eliot, and A. Lawrence Lowell. In addition, two other Unitarians exercised the office of president without the title: Henry Ware and Andrew Preston Peabody.

HORACE MANN

1796-1859

Courtesy of the Library of Congress

Born in poverty, Mann lived in hardship on the family farm in Franklin, Massachusetts. His schooling was limited to about three months a year. He had mastered the tenets of his family's Calvinistic faith by the age of ten, but when their minister condemned his dear drowned brother Stephen to eternal damnation, Horace rebelled and later became a Unitarian.

After receiving some private tutoring, he graduated from Brown University, studied law, and began his career first as a state representative and then as a Massachusetts senator. He was active in the establishment of a state mental hospital in Worcester. Nevertheless, Senator Mann abandoned his highly promising political career and, in 1837, accepted the position of his state's first secretary of the Board of Education. He encouraged the first Normal School for teachers. He advocated the establishment of free public libraries. State and local support to education soon doubled. In Mann's famous twelve annual reports, he insisted that it is necessary for the state to assume the responsibility to educate each child as a natural right. Compulsory school attendance began. Schools were now required to receive nonsectarian support through taxation.

In 1853, Horace Mann became the president of Antioch College in Ohio, implementing the ideal of coeducational, nonsectarian higher education. Raising funds weakened his health, but Antioch students heard these words shortly before his death: "Be ashamed to die before you have won some battle for humanity."

Mary Tyler Peabody Mann

1806-1887

Mary Mann and her youngest son, Benjy, in a photo from a family album

The wife of Horace Mann—and sister of Elizabeth Palmer Peabody and Sophia Peabody Hawthorne—was an educator who substantially assisted her husband. Her writing and editing included a novel, letters, a cookbook, early childhood education papers, and the *Life and Works of Horace Mann* in three volumes.

ELIZABETH PALMER PEABODY

1804-1894

Courtesy of Concord Magazine

Greatly esteemed in the 1800s as part of the intellectual elite in Boston—a member of the Transcendentalist inner circle, a prolific writer, and a leading educator—Elizabeth Palmer Peabody is best known today for promoting the kindergarten movement in the United States. Peabody's bonds with Unitarian minister William Ellery Channing were strong. He guided her reading in the 1820s and 1830s, and she later recorded his sermons. In 1834, she met Bronson Alcott. His Pennsylvania school had closed, and Peabody offered to help him establish a new school based on Transcendentalist ideas then current in Boston. Out of this association came a journal, *Record of a School*, which publicized Alcott's philosophy and projects.

Peabody was a serious scholar of religion and saw it as an essential part of education. She was drawn first to liberal Unitarianism and then to Transcendentalism, both of which stressed the goodness of humans, respect for nature, the responsibility to improve life on Earth, and the divine nature of each inner soul. For ten years, the foreign language bookstore she owned in Boston was a meeting place for such persons as Horace Mann (husband of her sister Mary), Nathaniel Hawthorne (husband of her sister Sophia), and

Theodore Parker. The bookstore also became a gathering place for leading women of the time, serving as the site for an important series of meetings for women referred to as "Conversations."

In her late fifties, Peabody was introduced to German educator Friedrich Froebel's ideas on early childhood education. She found them compatible with her own beliefs and is credited with opening the first English-speaking kindergarten in the United States in Boston in 1860. She spent the next thirty years establishing many such schools, training teachers, giving talks, and writing numerous articles and books on kindergarten theory and practices.

Abridged from a sketch by June Edwards in Standing Before Us: Unitarian Universalist Women and Social Reform 1776-1936, *edited by Dorothy May Emerson (Boston: Skinner House Books, 2000).*

BOOKER T. WASHINGTON

1856-1915

Courtesy of the Library of Congress

Though born a slave, Washington attended the Hampton Normal and Agricultural Institute in Virginia, working as a janitor before graduating to join the Institute's staff. In 1881, he became the first president of the Tuskegee Normal and Industrial Institute in Alabama, now Tuskegee University. Unitarians advance the work he did at Tuskegee. He was not a Unitarian.

AMORY DWIGHT MAYO

1823-1907

Courtesy of the Unitarian Universalist Association

After studying theology with Hosea Ballou and serving both Universalist and Unitarian churches in Gloucester, Massachusetts, and Cleveland, Albany, and Cincinnati, Mayo devoted four years to a ministry of education through fourteen of the sixteen Southern states. He concluded that women teach all scholastic levels better than men and that "the present opportunities for education are woefully inadequate for both races."

CHARLES WILLIAM ELIOT

1834-1926

Courtesy of the Unitarian Universalist Association

Charles's mother, Mary Lyman Eliot, was a descendant of Pilgrims who landed at Plymouth in 1631. His father was a treasurer of Harvard College and served as mayor of Boston. His wife inherited a small fortune, but in the panic of 1857, the family became impoverished.

When Charles was teaching mathematics and chemistry at Harvard College, his five-year appointment ended without reappointment. He married Ellen Peabody, and they stretched their savings to travel to Europe, where he visited leading universities. After he declined a highly remunerative offer as an industrial executive because he wanted to concentrate in the field of education, he accepted appointment as professor of chemistry, becoming part of the newly forming faculty of the Massachusetts Institute of Technology. Professor Eliot wrote two notable articles published in 1869 in the *Atlantic Monthly* calling for the reform of American universities.

In the same year, Eliot was astounded to be elected president of Harvard University by a close but nevertheless decisive vote. Four days later his wife died, leaving two motherless boys. He was inaugurated as Harvard's president in the meetinghouse of the First Church (Unitarian) in Cambridge, where he remained a member for life. Eliot worked closely with the presidents of Cornell and Johns Hopkins—Andrew White and Daniel Colt Gilman—to jointly create a viable structure of higher education in America.

President Eliot was patient and persistent in the face of opposition as he boldly labored to unify the education system. He also gained world renown for his service as a citizen. He is perhaps best remembered, other than for his presidency, for the five-foot-long series of fifty volumes in our libraries, *The Harvard Classics*, which he edited in retirement to advance education for people with a passion to learn.

WILLIAM GREENLEAF ELIOT

1811-1887

Members of William G. Eliot's church in St. Louis, Missouri organized an educational institute, which, in 1857, became Washington University. Its charter permitted no sectarianism in religion or politics. Three-quarters of the early financial support came from members of his Unitarian congregation. Eliot reluctantly became the university's first chancellor in 1871, and he therefore became minister *emeritus* of the church, which he had founded in 1834. At the time of his death in 1887, there were sixteen hundred students and one hundred faculty members teaching in Washington University's college and schools of law, medicine, dentistry, fine arts, and engineering.

This man of small stature and fragile health managed to pioneer jointly in a parish and community ministry in the West which he deliberately choose, determined upon graduating from Harvard Divinity School, "to remain and lay down my ashes in the valley of the Mississippi." Among Eliot's other achievements were functioning as a Unitarian Christian missionary in the world around St. Louis, facilitating the formation of economically viable public schools, acting to keep the state of Mississippi in the Union, and providing leadership in the creation of the Western Sanitary Commission hospital agencies in the West to attend to medical emergencies of Civil War soldiers.

In 1854 Harvard University honored him with the degree of Doctor of Divinity.

GEORGE TICKNOR

1791-1871

*Thomas Sully, 1828 portrait,
courtesy of the Dartmouth College Library*

After George—then only ten years old—was interviewed by the president of Dartmouth College, he was unconditionally admitted to the school.

After practicing law for one year and finding that occupation uncongenial, Ticknor studied in Germany and was then appointed a Harvard professor of French, Spanish, and *belles lettres*. Among his students were James Russell Lowell and Henry David Thoreau. When he resigned, his successor was Henry Wadsworth Longfellow.

His major achievement as a writer was his *History of Spanish Literature* in three volumes. His major public achievement was helping to establish the Boston Public Library. He wrote the initial planning report and in 1860 donated more than 2,400 of his own books. He served as president of the library's board of trustees.

John Lowell, Jr.

1799-1836

Francis Cabot Lowell, John's father, was the founder of cotton manufacturing in the United States. The Boston Manufacturing Company is considered the first large American manufacturing corporation, and the prototype for many more to come.

John was a sickly child who was not happy at Harvard, so he left after two years to travel to Indonesia and India. Upon returning, he worked with his father helping to finance the construction of huge cotton mills, as well as one of America's first railroads, the Boston and Lowell Line.

In 1830-1831, John Lowell lost both his wife and two daughters to scarlet fever. When he decided he would circle the earth, he sold his properties in order to establish an institute for popular education by offering lectures or courses for the public either free or with nominal charge. After two years of visiting Europe, he and a companion went to Egypt, where he suffered various illnesses before taking an utterly exhausting journey by camel across the desert. Although he was able to take a ship to India, he died three weeks after arriving in Bombay.

Immediately upon opening in 1838, the Lowell Institute—operated by the family with a single trustee—flourished. Thanks to the wise investment of the initial endowment of $250,000, the institute now cosponsors free public lectures, national weekly public radio broadcasts, international webcasts of the WGBH Forum Network, university extension courses at Harvard, and the cultural treasures of public television broadcasts via the WGBH Educational Foundation.

From *The Lowells and Their Seven Worlds* by Ferris Greenslet, The Riverside Press, 1946

7. Arts

DANIEL CHESTER FRENCH

1850-1931

French at work in his studio.
Courtesy of the Library of Congress

Ralph Waldo Emerson helped Daniel Chester French, America's best-known sculptor, secure his first big commission: the Minute Man statue in Concord celebrating the centennial of the first battle of the American Revolution. President Grant and 10,000 people attended its unveiling on April 19, 1875.

French created the statues of General Grant in Philadelphia, of General Washington in Paris, and of John Harvard in the Harvard Yard, Cambridge. Surpassing them all is the eighteen-foot-high marble revelation of Abraham Lincoln seated in quiet majesty in the Lincoln Memorial in Washington, D.C.

In 1969, French's daughter Margaret gave his estate, Chesterwood, to the National Trust for Historic Preservation. The studio of the Unitarian sculptor is open to the public at Stockbridge in the Berkshires.

Charles Bulfinch: Architect of the Capitol

1763-1844

The American architect was born in Boston, Massachusetts, the son of Thomas Bulfinch, a prominent and wealthy physician. He was educated at the Boston Latin School and at Harvard, where he graduated in 1781. After several years of travel and study in Europe, in 1787 he settled in Boston, where he was the first to practice as a professional architect. Among his early works were the old Federal Street theatre (1793), the first playhouse in New England, and the "new" State House (1798). He was chairman of the Board of Selectmen of Boston from 1797 to 1818. He provided for new systems of drainage and street lighting, reorganizing the police and fire departments, and straightening and widening the streets. He was one of the promoters in 1787 of the voyage of the ship "Columbia," which under the command of Captain Robert Gray (1755-1806) was the first to carry the American flag around the world. In 1818, Bulfinch succeeded B.H. Latrobe (1764-1820) as architect of the National Capitol at Washington. He completed the unfinished wings and central portion, constructing the rotunda from plans of his own after suggestions of his predecessor, and designed the new western approach and portico. In 1830, he returned to Boston, where he died on April 15, 1844.

From *Encyclopaedia Britannica*, 14th Edition, 1929

FANNY KEMBLE

1809-1893

*Photograph from a painting by Thomas Sully.
Courtesy of the Library of Congress*

Born in London as a member of a notable acting family, Kemble was able to prevent the family's financial ruin by studying acting for three weeks and making a sensational debut as Juliet in *Romeo and Juliet*. In 1832 she toured the United States and Canada, where she was praised as the first great actress on the North American stage.

After being courted by Pierce Butler, a Philadelphia gentleman from a slave-owning family with a Georgia plantation, she married him. The union bolstered her family's financial prospects, but conflicts were soon evident. Fanny Kemble had been influenced by Unitarian minister William Ellery Channing to seek the abolition of slavery. When she insisted on visiting the Georgia rice and cotton plantation, she was so horrified by what she saw that she wrote a journal of her experience; her husband demanded that she not publish it, as it was an act in disobedience to his will.

Distraught and seeking to recuperate, she left her husband and their two children and traveled to the Continent. He began divorce proceedings. She began public dramatic readings with great success. When she agreed not to testify about his unfaithfulness, she was granted two summer months each year with the children and $1,500 per year in alimony.

Pierce Butler squandered his inheritance through gambling and stock speculation. In 1861 he was arrested for treason and then released. His former slaves became his sharecroppers. After contracting malaria, he died in 1867.

Fanny Kemble died in London in 1893 after continuing her career of dramatic readings and publishing many writings, including her *Journal of a Residence on a Georgia Plantation.*

CHARLOTTE CUSHMAN

1816-1876

Courtesy of the Library of Congress

Charlotte's father was a descendant of Robert Cushman, one of the Pilgrims who landed at Plymouth in 1620.

She was a celebrated actress who triumphed in both the United States and Great Britain—the first native-born woman so honored. Although school ended for her at age thirteen, she learned much through her uncle's taking her to the Tremont Theatre in Boston, where both English and American actors performed. Friends advised Charlotte, "You are a born actress; go on the stage."

Charlotte Cushman was electrifying in playing both male and female roles—both Lady Macbeth and Hamlet! Ralph Waldo Emerson was her minister when she joined the Second Church (Unitarian) in Boston, where she sang in the choir.

Among her admirers were Thomas Carlyle, Henry Longfellow, Julia Ward Howe, and Fanny Kemble. In 1915, she was elected to the New York University Hall of Fame.

HARRIET HOSMER

1830-1905

Courtesy of the Library of Congress

This pioneer woman sculptor was a descendant of James Hosmer, who came from England to Massachusetts in the 1630s. After her mother died of tuberculosis when Harriet was four, her father encouraged her to lead an outdoor life. At Mrs. Charles Sedwick's School in the Berkshires, her Unitarian school classmates—novelist Catherine Maria Sedgwick and actress Fanny Kemble—suggested that she become a professional sculptor.

Medical schools then denied women students, but a friend of her physician father taught her anatomy. When she was studying in Rome, her overseer was actress Charlotte Cushman. John Gibson, an English sculptor, accepted her as his only student.

Of her many works, the amusing "Puck" playing on a toadstool was purchased by the Prince of Wales. Because of its popularity, she created fifty replicas that sold for $1,000 each. A colossal statue of Senator Thomas Hart Benton was commissioned by the state of Missouri. When Harriet's detractors claimed her work was done by male assistants, she brought a libel suit and wrote in defense an authoritative *Atlantic Monthly* article on "The Process of Sculpture."

Among the sculptor's many friends in Rome were Robert and Elizabeth Barrett Browning.

SAMUEL LONGFELLOW

1819-1892

Courtesy of CyberHymnal

Samuel's father was a member of the U.S. House of Representatives. His mother was a descendant of the John Alden and Priscilla of his brother Henry Wadsworth Longfellow's *Courtship of Miles Standish*. In college he began his lifelong friendship with Edward Everett Hale, and in the Divinity School began his long collaboration with his fellow hymn writer Samuel Johnson. Theodore Parker called their Book of Hymns the "Sam Book," which joyfully celebrated God's being really present with us.

After preaching his first two sermons—for which he received two dollars—Longfellow was ordained and served in Fall River, Massachusetts, and then in Brooklyn, New York, where his innovation of vesper services was the occasion for his writing the long-beloved hymns, "Now on Land and Sea Descending" and "Again as Evening Shadows Fall."

In addition to his composing various poems, hymns, and essays, Samuel Longfellow wrote the *Life of Henry Wadsworth Longfellow*.

8. Science

MARIA MITCHELL

1818-1889

When Vassar College opened in 1865 and the trustees voted to allow women faculty, Maria Mitchell accepted their offer. Athough she had never had any higher education, she had attended a school for young ladies conducted by an educational pioneer—the Unitarian minister Cyrus Peirce.

She was born on Nantucket Island. There, she and her banker father made observations of the stars through a U.S. Coast Survey telescope. Although she retained Quaker connections, she attended the Unitarian Church on the island.

In 1847, she made the first telescopic discovery of a planet and won a gold medal from the king of Denmark. Her role as a scientist extended into the entire scientific community. Maria Mitchell helped organize the Association for the Advancement of Science, subsequently becoming its first woman member in 1850. She also was elected to the American Academy of Arts and Sciences.

From Maria Mitchell: *Life, Letters, and Journals*, 1896

JOSEPH PRIESTLEY

1733-1804

History remembers Priestley as a scientist (he discovered oxygen in 1774), author, and clergyman. Priestley probably would have reversed the order, giving first priority to his work as a minister. Earl Morse Wilbur pronounced him "beyond doubt the most infuential figure in the earlier history of the Unitarian movement in England."

Educated at a Dissenting academy, Priestley found himself on the heretical side of most theological questions. As a young minister and teacher he studied the Scriptures only to find, like Servetus before him, that they provided meager support for the doctrines of the Church, notably the Trinity and the atonement (i.e., the belief that through the death and resurrection of Jesus Christ men's sins are forgiven and divine justice is satisfied). He later described his pilgrimage as a "passing from Trinitarianism to high Arianism, from this to low Arianism, and from this to Socinianism."

Priestley's intellectual brilliance and broad interests attracted to him some of the finest thinkers of his age, including Benjamin Franklin, Thomas Jefferson, and Richard Price.

His main contribution to English Unitarianism was a comprehensive argument, both historical and philosophical, for liberal Christianity—drawn from Scripture and the Christian fathers, interpreted by reason, and rigorously applied to the religious and political problems of his day. "Absurdity supported by power," he wrote, "will never be able to stand its ground against the efforts of reason."

Of all of Priestley's religious works, probably the most infuential was his *History of the Corruptions of Christianity* in two volumes, in which he sought to show that true Christianity, embodied in the beliefs of the primitive church, was Unitarian, and that all departures from that faith were corruptions. The Corruptions infuriated the orthodox and delighted the liberals in both England and America. It was publicly burned in Holland.

From *The Epic of Unitarianism* by David B. Parke (Boston: Beacon Press, 1957).

LOUIS AGASSIZ

1807-1873

Courtesy of the Library of Congress

The fourteenth edition of the *Encyclopedia Britannica* (1929) notes that Louis Agassiz was a Swiss-American naturalist and geologist whose catalog (of all the names applied to all the genera of animals) had a practical value that can hardly be overestimated. His study of glaciers was the most important of all his works, which included *Lake Superior* (1850) and *Contribution to the Natural History of the United States*. As a professor of zoology at Harvard, he was the ablest scientist America had known. He said, "The book of nature is always open. Strive to interpret what really exists." His attitude toward Darwinism all his lifetime was cold and unsympathetic.

NATHANIEL BOWDITCH

1773-1838

Courtesy of the Peabody Essex Museum

When his father—a shipmaster in Salem, Massashusetts—faced financial troubles, Nathaniel's formal education ended. Self-education continued on his five voyages on merchant ships destined for India and Europe.

After becoming the head of the Essex Fire and Marine Insurance Company in Salem in 1804, Bowditch became, until his death, actuary of the Massachusetts Hospital Life Insurance Company. Because this position provided him time for research and writing, he declined election as professor of mathematics and philosophy at Harvard, as well as offers from West Point and the University of Virginia.

His publications include *The New American Practical Navigator* (1802), still used for sea navigation, and his translation and annotation of La Place's five-volume summary of the progress of astronomy, *Traite de Mechanique Celeste.*

He was elected as a foreign member of the Royal Society of London, president of the American Academy of Arts and Sciences, and Fellow of the Harvard Corporation.

BENJAMIN ATHROP GOULD

1824-1896

Dr. Gould, born in Boston, was the first American to obtain a Ph.D. in Astronomy from Germany (Göttingen). His commitment to professionalize American astronomy included the founding and editing of *The Astronomical Journal* beginning in 1849.

While now celebrated primarily for his enormous accomplishment of mapping 32,000 stars of the Southern Heavens, Gould also made the first determinations of the trans-Atlantic latitudes by telegraph; organized meteorological stations from the tropics to Tierra del Fuego and from the Andes to the Atlantic; pioneered in the use of the camera as an instrument of precision; and was one of the founders of the National Academy of Sciences.

JAMES JACKSON, MD: MEDICAL SCIENCE PIONEER

1777-1867

Massachusetts General Hospital, Boston

At the beginning of the nineteenth century, Boston had no hospital for the treatment of general disease, though there were such institutions in New York and Philadelphia. For many years there were various indications in the community that the want of such an establishment was beginning to be felt; in the summer of 1810 strenuous efforts were made to supply the want, which proved successful. A circular-letter, dated August 20, 1810, was prepared by Dr. James Jackson and Dr. John Collins Warren, and addressed to some of the most influential citizens of Boston and its neighborhood, for the purpose of awakening in their minds an interest in the subject. It was the opinion of Mr. Bowditch, as recorded in his History of the Massachusetts General Hospital, that this circular-letter might be regarded as the cornerstone of the institution.

Dr. James Jackson, the first signer, is perhaps the most conspicuous character in the medical annals of Massachusetts. No physician in the Commonwealth ever exerted so large and lasting an influence over his professional brethren or his patients. Born in Newburyport on October 3, 1777, Jackson graduated from Harvard College in the class of 1796, and went on to study his profession under the venerable Dr. Holyoke of Salem. In the year 1812 he was appointed to the Hershey Professorship of the Theory and Practice of Medicine, which he continued to hold until 1836. At that time he gave up the active duties of the office and was chosen professor *emeritus*. His writings are numerous, and all his publications show great wisdom as well as literary culture. During a period of more than half a century he was a frequent contributor to the pages of the *New England Journal of Medicine and Surgery,* and of the *Boston Medical and Surgical Journal.*

By Samuel A. Green, *Memorial History of Boston, 1630-1880,* Volume IV, 1883

JEFFRIES WYMAN: NATURALIST

1814-1874

William James considered Jeffries Wyman "an exemplar of the scientific life." In cooperation with his colleagues, Loius Agassiz and Asa Gray, Wyman is noted for making Harvard America's most distinguished center for the study of natural history. In addition to his teaching of comparative anatomy, he initiated the Museum of Comparative Anatomy, using his private collection, and was also the first curator of the Peabody Museum of Archaelogy and Ethnology. In contrast to Louis Agassiz, he was sympathetic to evolution, as were Asa Gray of Harvard and both William Barton Rogers, the founder of the Massachusetts Institute of Technology, and his brother, Henry Darwin Rogers.

ASAPH HALL:
DISCOVERER OF THE MOONS OF MARS

1829-1907

Courtesy of the Mars Society, Toronto

Born in Goshen, Connecticut, and educated largely at home by his father, Hall became an apprentice carpenter at the age of thirteen after both of his parents died. After studying one year at the University of Michigan at Ann Arbor, his passion for geometry and algebra led him to become an assistant at the Harvard College Observatory. He then had a wife, $25 in cash, and a salary of $3 a week.

When he left in 1863 for the U.S. Naval Observatory, he was in charge of its great refractor, located at Foggy Bottom on the banks of the Potomac River in Washington, DC. In 1878 he saw a "a faint star near Mars" which turned out to be outer and inner satellites of Mars. Hall named them Phobos (Fear) and Deimos (Flight) after the attendants of Mars mentioned in Homer's Iliad, and he measured their mass in comparison with Earth (0.1076 percent). Word came from the Paris Observatory that this was "one of the most important discoveries of modern astronomy." In 1879, Hall was presented the Gold Medal of the Royal Astronomical Society of Great Britain.

BENJAMIN PEIRCE

1809-1880

From *The Harvard Book*, Volume I, 1875

A professor of mathematics, astronomy, and natural philosophy at Harvard from 1833 until his death, Peirce also served as superintendent of the United States Coast Survey, for which he created a general map of the United States.

He authored many articles and eleven books, thereby centering America's mathematics and astronomical research at Harvard University. He also helped to organize the Smithsonian Institution and to incorporate the National Academy of Science.

His son, Charles Sanders Peirce, initiated the American philosophy known as pragmatism.

PERCIVAL LOWELL

1855-1916

Percival Lowell, an astronomer, was a member of a Boston Unitarian family, which included his older brother, A. Lawrence Lowell, who became president of Harvard, and his sister, Amy Lowell, the Imagist poet. Upon graduating from Harvard College where he excelled in mathematics, Percival Lowell visited Japan and Korea. He not only traveled but also played a diplomatic role and wrote four books about East Asia.

Shifting his interests to astronomy, he established the Lowell Observatory in Flagstaff, Arizona in 1894, and in 1895 wrote the first of his three books about the planet Mars. Although Lowell mistakenly concluded that Mars displayed evidence of intelligent beings, he awakened wide popular interest in the planet, including fantasy literature, *War of the Worlds* by H. G. Wells in 1898, as well as a riot inducing 1938 radio broadcast declaring *Invasion from Mars* by Orson Wells.

In 1975, spacecrafts Viking 1 and Viking 2 were launched to study Mars, the longest-surviving active laboratories on the surface of another world.

Although Percival Lowell did not live to see the reliable scientific evidence fulfilling his mathematical prediction of a planet beyond Neptune, Pluto was discovered in 1930.

9. Business

ABBOTT LAWRENCE

1792-1855

Courtesy of the Lawrence Heritage State Park

The younger brother of Amos Lawrence was a businessman, diplomat, and philanthropist whose father fought at Bunker Hill.

While a partner with his brother in founding the firm of A. and A. Lawrence, he also engaged in fostering industrial development and was an early advocate of railroad extension from Boston and Worcester to Albany. The town of Lawrence, Massachusetts, is named in his honor.

In 1834, Abbott Lawrence was elected to the U.S. House of Representatives and served on the Ways and Means Committee. In 1849 he was U.S. ambassador to the Court of St. James.

When he died in 1855, his estate included bequests for model housing for the poor, as well as an endowment for the Lawrence Scientific School at Harvard. The original school has been succeeded by the strikingly modern Undergraduate Science Center designed in the same location by the office of L. J. Sert in 1970.

AMOS LAWRENCE

1786-1852

Courtesy of Lawrence University, Appleton, Wisconsin

Amos Lawrence, American merchant and philanthropist, was a descendant of one of the first settlers of Groton, Massachusetts. After establishing his own business in Boston, he and his brother Abbott became partners in A. and A. Lawrence. Their firm did much to establish the textile industry in America. In 1831, Amos retired from active business, and Abbott was thereafter the head of the firm—the greatest American mercantile house of the day.

Deciding in 1842 not to add to his property, Amos became a benefactor of such educational institutions as Williams College, Kenyon College, and Lawrence Academy. He established the Boston Children's Infirmary and aided the building of the Bunker Hill Monument.

ENOCH PRATT

1808-1896

Courtesy of the Enoch Pratt Free Library

Enoch Pratt's first American ancestor on his father's side arrived in Massachusetts in 1628; on his mother's side, in 1662. When his formal education ended at the age of fifteen, he moved to Baltimore and began his business career by selling nails and mule shoes before moving into transportation, insurance, and banking. From 1860 until his death, he was the president of the National Farmers' and Planters' Bank of Baltimore. Pratt also became president of the Baltimore Clearing House and the Maryland Bankers' Association, in addition to establishing a role in several transportation companies.

Enoch Pratt and his wife had no children. He dedicated his growing wealth to civic improvement in Baltimore. Indeed, he became a great philanthropist like two other Baltimore Unitarians: Johns Hopkins and George Peabody. After building a free central library and four branch libraries, he granted the city $833,333.31 to assure that the library that he'd given the city would always be free to all. At the beginning of the twenty-first century, there are more than twenty-five branches of the Enoch Pratt Free Library. Andrew Carnegie was so impressed that he began libraries in other cities, declaring, "Pratt was my pioneer."

JONAS G. CLARK

1815-1900

Courtesy of Clark University

Jonas Clark founded Clark University in Worcester, Massachusetts, on eight acres of land on Main Street across from the previously established University Park. The Massachusetts State Legislature granted a charter on January 18, 1887. The cornerstone of the first building was laid on October 22, 1887. The first president, installed on January 18, 1887, was G. Stanley Hall, a professor at John Hopkins.

On June 21, 1905, when President Theodore Roosevelt arrived in Worcester, he was escorted from Union Station to Clark University by a large military parade. After addressing the gathering, he had dinner at the home of Rockwood Hoar, the son of Senator Hoar.

Jonas Clark, a citizen who by enterprise and the exercise of great native ability grew wealthy, founded an institution designed to enlarge the boundaries of human knowledge. His first grant of $2,000,000 was for philosophical research, to be extended in all directions. He later contributed an additional $2,000,000.

HARRISON GRAY OTIS

1765-1848

*Portrait by Gilbert Stuart, 1809
Courtesy of the Society for the Preservation
of New England Antiquities*

This Unitarian businessman and lawyer was appointed by George Washington as a U.S. district attorney for Massachusetts and served as one of the original incorporators of the Boston Bank. A strong advocate for centralized government, Otis warned that Napoleon's mounting victories might "roll toward our shores."

His public service included terms in both the U.S. House of Representatives (1797-1801) and the Massachusetts state legislature (1802-1817). He was the primary actor in the controversial Hartford Convention of 1814, a gathering that favored states' rights. From 1817 to 1822 Otis served as a U.S. senator, returning to Boston in 1829 to serve as its mayor.

The elegant Harrison Gray Otis House in Boston is now the home of the Society for the Preservation of New England Antiquities.

PETER COOPER

1791-1883

Courtesy of the Library of Congress

Born in New York City, this inventor, manufacturer, and philanthropist had only one year of formal education. After being apprenticed to a coach maker, he made machines for shearing cloth and then perfected and patented a cloth-cutter that he manufactured. When he purchased a glue factory and improved its quality, it became a major source of his wealth. After purchasing a plot on the Baltimore harbor, he discovered rich iron ore on the property, then founded the Canton Iron Works, which increased his fortune.

Peter Cooper designed the first steam locomotive built in America and called it "Tom Thumb." He and Cyrus Field laid the first Atlantic cable.

He became the president of the North American Telegraph Company, which controlled most U.S. telegraph lines.

Peter Cooper fought for free public schools and vigorously opposed the use of public funds to support Roman Catholic schools. He ran unsuccessfully for president of the United States.

He is best remembered as the founder of the Cooper Union in New York City, a school long celebrated for featuring free courses in the arts and sciences.

Cooper and his family were members of All Souls Unitarian Church, New York.

JOHN MURRAY FORBES: RAILROAD PIONEER AND ABOLITIONIST

1813-1898

Born in Bordeaux, France, and raised in Milton, Massachusetts, Forbes faced his father's death when he was six. At the age of twelve he entered the family business as a clerk in the China counting-house of his uncles. Five years later he "shipped before the mast" to Canton, replacing his brother Tom, who had died while serving as an agent for Houqua, China's leading export merchant. By learning quickly and acquiring an early fortune, he returned home and married, but soon sailed back alone to China, in three years gaining what was then great wealth, $100,000.

Upon returning to the United States, John Forbes left the volatile China trade and invested in land, iron, and railroads. While actively participating in the Saturday Club with Boston Unitarians notable in science, religion, philosophy, and literature, Forbes was president of the Chicago Central Railroad, which pioneered the first trains from the East to Chicago. Throughout half a century of investing in the consolidation of railroad development opening the West, he led in the creation of the newly industrializing nation's very first big business. He is recognized as a pioneering precursor of Henry Ford a century later.

John Murray Forbes, long admired by many for his personal integrity, contributed to American society through endorsing Wendell Phillips, providing weapons to fight slavery, and entertaining John Brown. In addition to providing wartime counsel to President Lincoln and his cabinet, Forbes was sent on a secret mission to England that prevented the Confederacy from securing two ironclad ships. Among his various other philanthropies were his help in building the Massachusetts Institute of Technology, as well as the Tuskegee and Hampton Schools, and his lead in fostering the Robert Gould Shaw monument on the Boston Common just across from the Unitarian Universalist Association on Beacon Street.

From *Famous Families of Massachusetts*, Vol. 1, by Mary Caroline Crawford, Boston, 1930.

Thomas H. Perkins: Merchant Prince of Boston

1764-1854

Born in Boston, Colonel Perkins grew up during the American Revolution and, as a boy, witnessed the Boston Massacre of 1770. In 1786 he and his brother James became commission merchants engaged in foreign trade of anything profitable, including tea, silk, spices, slaves and opium. A massive fortune resulted from the shipping business with China and from his many investments at home: mining, quarrying, hotels, and America's first railway.

Acquaintance with George Washington was a part of Perkins's experience in state and national politics, which included leadership in the state militia corps. Today he is primarily honored for his philanthropies: the Boston Atheneum, the Massachusetts General Hospital, the Bunker Hill Monument, and the Perkins Institute for the Blind. His affiliation with the First Parish in Brookline betokens his Unitarian faith.

A biography published by Harvard University Press, coauthored by Unitarian Universalist minister Carl Seaburg, is *Merchant Prince of Boston: Colonel T. H. Perkins, 1764-1854.*

From *The Memorial History of Boston, 1630-1880*

Ezra Cornell

1807-1874

The entrepreneur who founded Cornell University was the son of Quaker parents in the Bronx. His father, who had been a potter and a schoolteacher, purchased a farm in upstate New York. Cornell became a journeyman carpenter and then a foreman of a grain and wall plaster mill. When Cornell married an Episcopalian, Mary Ann Wood, he was excommunicated by the Quaker meeting.

Cornell's farm was a model for others. He invented and patented a special farm plow. When Samuel F.B. Morse invented the telegraph and sought to transmit between Washington, D.C., and Baltimore, Ezra Cornell devised a way the first message could be communicated in 1844: "What hath God wrought?" He then supervised building a line between Albany and New York City. His stock price arose dramatically, making him wealthy.

Ezra Cornell served a term in the New York state legislature. He donated $100,000 toward creating a free public library in Ithaca. He proposed that New York act under the Morrill Act to provide instruction in agriculture and mechanic arts in Ithaca, with Andrew D. White serving as the first president of Cornell. He provided an endowment of $500,000. Admission was open to rich and poor, without any religious restrictions, and was open to both male and female students as early as 1872.

ENDNOTE

The Beacon on Beacon Hill

The story of the historic beacon is reliably told as follows by Justin Winsor, the librarian of Harvard College, in volume one of his four-volume *Memorial History of Boston, 1630-1880*, published in 1880.

> The beacon on the hill—in the foreground is the original wooden Kings Chapel. In 1634 the General Court ordered that the fort at Boston erect for defence on the waterside a beacon to be fired upon the discovery of any danger.
>
> The beacon on Sentry Hill was the great alarm-tower of the town. It was ordered to be set up in March, 1634, to give notice to the country of any danger, and that there shall be a ward of one person kept there from the first of April to the last of September, and that upon the discovery of any danger the beacon shall be fired, an alarm given, as well as also messengers presently sent by that town where the danger is discovered to all other towns within the jurisdiction. Later, in 1645, it was ordered that all the youth from ten to sixteen years should be instructed by a competent person in the exercise of small arms, such as small guns, half pikes, and bows and arrows.
>
> The beacon…was simply a tall pole furnished with wooden rungs for climbing, with an iron pot filled with tar depending from a crane at its top.
>
> It is not known if the combustibles were ever fired. Flaming from a height of sixty-five feet from the ground, and over two hundred above the tide, the beacon would have furnished a conspicuous signal in case of alarm.
>
> After the erection of the beacon in 1635 it received the name of Beacon Hill.

Alphabetical Index of Names

Adams, Abigail 34
Adams, Charles Francis 39
Adams, John 33
Adams, John Quincy 37
Agassiz, Louis 172
Alcott, Louisa May 68
Arminius, Jacobus 31
Anthony, Susan B. 127
Ballou, Hosea 27
Bancroft, Aaron 93
Bancroft, George 60
Belknap, Jeremy 23
Bellows, Henry Whitney 107
Bentley, William 24
Bergh, Henry 138
Blackwell, Antoinette B. 115
Bowditch, Nathaniel 173
Buckminister, Joseph S. 30
Bulfinch, Charles 162
Calvin, John 7
Calhoun, John 53
Channing, William Ellery 85
Chauncy, Charles 19
Child, Lydia 81
Choate, Joseph Hodges 47
Clark, Jonas G. 186
Clarke, James Freeman 100
Collyer, Robert 108
Cooper, Peter 188
Cornell, Ezra 193
Crothers, Samuel M. 112
Curtis, George W. 75
Cushman, Charlotte 166
Dall, Charles 142
Dix, Dorothea 139
Edwards, Jonathan 18
Eliot, Charles W. 153
Eliot, Samuel Atkins 124
Eliot, Thomas Lamb 121
Eliot, William G. 155
Emerson, Ralph Waldo 63
Emerson, William 29
Everett, Charles C. 119
Everett, Edward 49
Fields, James T. 72
Fillmore, Millard 41
Fiske, John 82
Follen, Charles 102
Forbes, John Murray 190
Freeman, James 26
French, Daniel C. 161
Frothingham, Octavius B. . . .116
Fuller, Margaret 77
Gannett, Ezra Stiles 113

Gannett, William C. 120
Gay, Ebenezer 21
Gould, Benjamin A. 174
Hale, Edward Everett 97
Hall, Asaph 178
Harte, Bret 76
Harvard Univ. Presidents 145
Hawthorne, Nathaniel 70
Hedge, Frederic Henry 104
Hildreth, Richard 80
Hoar, George F. 57
Holmes, Oliver Wendell 67
Holmes, Jr., Oliver Wendell 48
Hosmer, Harriet 167
Howe, Julia Ward 128
Howe, Samuel Gridley 137
Jackson, James 175
Jefferson, Thomas 40
Jones, Jenkin Lloyd 110
Kemble, Fanny 164
King, Thomas Starr 96
Lawrence, Abbott 183
Lawrence, Amos 184
Longfellow, Henry W. 65
Longfellow, Samuel 168
Lowell, Jr., John 158
Lowell, Josephine Shaw 134
Lowell, Percival 180
Mann, Horace 146
Mann, Mary 148
May, Samuel J. 141
Mayhew, Jonathan 20
Mayo, Amory Dwight 152
Mead, Edwin D. 136
Melville, Herman 73
Mitchell, Maria 169
Morrill, Justin S. 58
Otis, Harrison Gray 187
Parker, Theodore 88
Parkman, Francis 83
Parsons, Theophilus 43
Peabody, Andrew 105
Peabody, Elizabeth P. 149
Peabody, Francis G. 117
Peirce, Benjamin 179
Perkins, Thomas H. 192
Pickering, Timothy 44
Pierpont, John 99
Pilgrims, The 11
Pratt, Enoch 185
Prescott, William H. 84
Priestley, Joseph 170
Quincy, Josiah 56
Ripley, Ezra 25
Robinson, John 12
Safford, Mary 93
Saltonstall, Sir Richard 15
Shaw, Robert Gould 55
Sparks, Jared 87
Stanton, Elizabeth C. 125
Stone, Lucy 130
Story, Joseph 46
Sumner, Charles 51
Sunderland, Jabez T. 143
Ticknor, George 157
Tuckerman, Joseph 132
Vane, Henry 14
Ware, Jr., Henry 90
Ware, Sr., Henry 89
Ware, William 79
Washington, Booker T. . . .151
Webster, Daniel 52
West, Samuel 22
Williams, Roger 16
Winthrop, John 13
Worcester, Noah 28
Wyman, Jeffries 177

Printed in the United States
33017LVS00010B/52